## JACK SHEPHERD

Jack Shepherd was born in Leeds. He studied art at King's College, Newcastle, after which he went to Central School of Speech and Drama in London and was a student founder of the Drama Centre. He has since enjoyed a successful career as a stage actor, at the Royal Court Theatre and the National Theatre, as well as being well known for his role in the popular BBC detective series *Wycliffe*. His television writing credits include *The Actual Woman*, *Underdog* and *Clapperjaw* (all for the BBC).

As a theatre writer, Jack has been involved in devised productions since the 1960s, such as *The Incredible Journey of Sir Francis Younghusband* (Royal Court Theatre Upstairs); *The Sleep of Reason* (Traverse Theatre, Edinburgh); and *Real Time* (a Joint Stock production). His plays *In Lambeth* (which he also directed at London's Donmar Theatre), and *Chasing the Moment* (Edinburgh Fringe Festival and Battersea Arts Centre) both won *Time Out* Awards for writing and directing, in 1989 and 1995 respectively. Jack's other plays include *Comic Cuts* (Derby Playhouse, Salisbury Theatre and Lyric Hammersmith Studio, 1995); *Half Moon* (Southwark Playhouse, 1998); and *Through a Cloud* (Drum Theatre, Plymouth and Birmingham Repertory Theatre, 2004, and Arcola Theatre, London, 2005), which is also published by Nick Hern Books.

Jack has previously directed three productions at Shakespeare's Globe, *The Two Gentlemen of Verona*, Thomas Dekker's *The Honest Whore*, and a mask play, *Man Falling Down. Holding Fire* is the third of his 'revolution' plays, following *In Lambeth*, a confrontation between William Blake and Tom Paine, and *Through a Cloud*, in which Oliver Cromwell and John Milton look back on the broken dreams of the English revolution.

Jack Shepherd

# HOLDING FIRE

**NICK HERN BOOKS**

London

www.nickhernbooks.co.uk

**A Nick Hern Book**

*Holding Fire* first published in Great Britain as a paperback original in 2007 by Nick Hern Books Limited, 14 Larden Road, London W3 7ST

*Holding Fire* © 2007 Jack Shepherd

Cover Design: Ned Hoste, 2H
Cover image: detail from 'The Race', from the series 'London, A Pilgrimage' (1872) by Paul-Gustave Dore and William Blanchard Jerrold, engraved by Bourguignon © Central St Martins School of Art and Design / The Bridgeman Art Library

Typeset by Country Setting, Kingsdown, Kent CT14 8ES
Printed and bound in Great Britain by Biddles, King's Lynn

A CIP catalogue record for this book is available from the British Library

ISBN 978 1 85459 998 8

*Holding Fire* was first performed at Shakespeare's Globe
Theatre, London, on 28 July 2007, with the following company:

Kirsty Besterman
Philip Bird
Cornelius Booth
Jim Bywater
Louise Callaghan
Philip Cumbus
Leander Deeny
Craig Gazey
Alice Haig
Peter Hamilton Dyer
Adam Kay
Jennifer Kidd
Pippa Nixon
Jonathan Moore
Christopher Obi
Dale Rapley
Mark Rice-Oxley
Nicholas Shaw

*Director*    Mark Rosenblatt
*Designer*    Janet Bird
*Music*    John Tams and Joe Townsend

# HOLDING FIRE

## Jack Shepherd

## Characters

LEADING CHARTISTS
**WILLIAM LOVETT**
**FEARGUS O'CONNOR**
**HENRY VINCENT**

THE ESTABLISHMENT
**COUNT D'ORSAY**
**IRA FREDERICK ALDRIDGE**
**OLIVER WADHAM**
**LORD JOHN RUSSELL**, *the Home Secretary*
**GENERAL SIR CHARLES NAPIER**

IN 'THE ROOKERIES'
**LIZZIE BAINS**, *a flower seller*
**MR BAINS**, *Lizzie's father*
**MRS BAINS**, *Lizzie's mother*
**BETH BAINS**, *a watercress seller, Lizzie's younger sister*
**SAM BAINS**, *Lizzie's younger brother*

AT THE BLACK LAMB TAVERN
**CHAS VELLINS**, *the landlord*
**MRS KETTLE**, *a whore*
**OLD JACK**, *an ancient Luddite*
**FRIEDRICH ENGELS**, *a German student*
**TOMKINS**, *a costermonger*

AT THE BULL AND MOUTH, THE COACHING INN
**PORTER**
**CLERK**
**COACHMAN**
**COACHMAN'S WIFE**
**THIN GIRL**

THE HARRINGTON HOUSEHOLD
**ARTHUR HARRINGTON**, *an industrialist*
**MRS HARRINGTON**, *his wife*
**BARRACLOUGH**, *the butler*

ELI MORGAN, *the cook*
MRS BURGESS, *the housekeeper*
JENKINS, *Mrs Harrington's manservant*
MOLLY, *the chambermaid*
DOROTHY, *the kitchen maid*
WILL, *the boot boy*
SIGNOR CAVELLINI, *a castrati tenor*
MAID
*Also various other servants*

IN THE FACTORY
RICHARD DENNISON, *a financier*
THOMAS GOODE, *a financier*
WEAVER
BOY

ROYALTY
YOUNG PRINCESS VICTORIA
PRINCE ALBERT OF SAXE COBURG GOTHA
*Two of Victoria's* LADIES-IN-WAITING
*Several members of* ALBERT'S FAMILY

AT THE PRIZE FIGHT
BURKE, *a deaf bare-knuckle fighter*
BENDIGO, *a bare-knuckle fighter*
REFEREE
BURKE'S SECONDS
DOCTOR

AT KERSAL MOOR
SAMUEL THOMPSON, *a Chartist organiser*
GUN CREW
OFFICER
GUNNER
SERGEANT
BLENKIRON, *a haulier*

AT THE CONVENTION
PETER BUSSEY, *a publican from Leeds*
JOHN DEEGAN, *a weaver from Lancashire*
ROBERT LOWERY, *a tailor from Newcastle*
JOHN WOLSTENHOME, *a file-maker from Sheffield*
CHAIRMAN

WARWICK JAIL
**MARY LOVETT**, *Lovett's wife*
**SAUNDERS**, *a prison guard*
**PRISON GUARD**
**CONVICT**
**PRISONERS**

NEWPORT
**ZEPHANIAH WILLIAMS**, *a Chartist Leader*
**JOHN FROST**, *a Chartist Leader*
**JOHN PHILLIPS**, *Mayor of Newport*
**SPECIAL CONSTABLE HATTERSLY**
**WELSH WOMAN**
**LIEUTENANT GRAY**
**MARCHERS**
**RED COATS**

IN THE PRISON
**JEREMY**, *Beth's boyfriend*
**OLD DEBTOR**
**OLD LADY**
**PRISON GOVERNOR**
**PRIEST**
**PRISON OFFICER**
**HANGMAN**

*Also*
**WORKING MAN**
**CROSSING SWEEPER**
**LORD MAYOR OF LONDON**
**SINGING PRISONER**

*As well as various well-dressed working men, stable hands, guests at the Harringtons' recital, working men, waiters, street musicians, marching and military bands, and crowds at various gatherings and meetings.*

*The stage directions in the text relate specifically to the play's original production at Shakespeare's Globe Theatre, and should therefore be adapted for the conditions and staging requirements of subsequent productions. See also Author's Note on page 115.*

## PART ONE

### Prologue

*London, 1837. The courtyard of The Crown and Anchor.*

WILLIAM LOVETT *enters through the central doors, accompanied by a scattering of well-dressed* WORKING MEN.

LOVETT. Before we adjourn upstairs for the serious business of the evening, I'd just like to draw your attention to the fact that our organisation is one year old today.

*Scattered applause.*

Casting my eye around, I notice that most of you have taken advantage of the facilities provided by this excellent hostelry. So let's raise our glasses in a toast, brothers . . . The London Working Men's Association!

*The* MEN *behind him raise their glassses. Mumbling: 'The London Working Men's Association.'*

One year old today! I tell you, it does my heart proud.

WORKING MAN. Are you sure you don't want something stronger, Bill?

LOVETT. No, thank you. This is nourishment enough for me.

*He drinks his water.*

In the summer of 1836 – just one year ago, brothers – we launched this frail craft of ours out onto a stormy sea. 'It'll never float,' they told us. 'In a month or two you'll have sunk without trace.' Well, more fool them, that's all I can say. Not only are we still afloat, brothers, but we're getting stronger and more seaworthy as every day goes by.

*People start drifting into the yard. A* CROSSING SWEEPER, *a couple of* STREET MUSICIANS, LIZZIE *and* BETH

BAINS *and* TOMKINS.

Thanks to our Association, folk are at last beginning to understand that there's nothing inevitable, preordained or in any way God-given about the nature of the society we live in. It's no longer an excuse for a man to plead ignorance and say: 'I don't know what those chaps in Parliament are up to, it's all beyond me.' Because here at the London Working Man's Association, he can bloody well come and find out!

*Enthusiastic applause.*

Here you can read books. Newspapers. Have them read to you if you can't make sense of the print. Listen to our speakers. Debate the greatest issues of the day. And in time, brethren, we'll have our own leaders; you mark my words, born into our *own* class, the labouring class. As well informed as any in the land.

TOMKINS. Twopence a pound, grapes! Penny a lot, fine Cox's.

LOVETT. And as fit to take the reins as any of those 'enlightened' gentlemen living up on Highgate Hill and in Hampstead's altogether sweeter air!

LIZZIE. Violets! Who'll buy my sweet violets?

LOVETT. But let's not get too carried away. All we've done so far is to take the first step on a long and perilous road. And in case you need reminding, it's a journey we're going to have to undertake alone. What we must learn, brothers, is to take the reins into our own hands. It would be folly, sheer folly, to expect any help from a class which has had its foot on our neck for the past hundred years and more. Oh, yes . . . it's true, we've been given promises. But what have these promises amounted to other than a carrot dangled in front of a flagging donkey? All they did in '32 was to give the vote to them with the property and the means, and leave the rest of us – as per usual – out in the cold. Saying: 'Shove your hands in your pockets, turn your face into the wind and bloody well get on with it.'

*A man crosses the yard, as if carefully picking his way along the filthy pavement. His clothes are lavish and by today's standards quite extraordinary: the epitome of high fashion. His name is* COUNT D'ORSAY; *under one arm he carries a large drawing book, wrapped in brown paper.*

BETH. Creases! Four bunch a penny! Get your water creases here.

*The child's voice is harsh and mechanical. As if she has no idea what the words mean.*

LOVETT. As things stand now, we're strangers in our own land.

*It's getting harder for* LOVETT. *The sounds of the street traders are beginning to unsettle his audience.*

TOMKINS. Now's your time. Collies, three for twopence. Penny a lot, fine Cox's.

LOVETT. Without rights! Without representation! A race apart!

LIZZIE. Violets! Who'll buy my sweet violets?

D'ORSAY *considers crossing the road.*

CROSSING SWEEPER. Hold up a moment while I attend to the crossing, sir. It has been most notoriously fouled since I last give it a sweep.

*The* CROSSING SWEEPER *strides out into the road and clears a pathway through the rubbish.*

LOVETT. I think it's time we adjourned upstairs, gentlemen. And conducted the business of the evening in more convivial circumstances.

*He retreats through the central doors, followed by the remaining L.W.M.A. members.*

CROSSING SWEEPER. We had a nag keeled over here this morning. A poor spavined creature it was, sir, pulling a load too heavy for her frail legs to bear. Dead afore she struck the cobbles.

*He gives a sign that* D'ORSAY *should cross.*

Still. It's all grist to the mill, ain't it, sir?

D'ORSAY. I am most grateful for your solicitude.

*When he reaches the other side, he searches in his purse.*

But if you were hoping for a handsome gratuity, it would be wise to remember that the splendour of the garment is no true indication of the solvency of the wearer.

*He finds a suitable coin and hands it to the* CROSSING SWEEPER.

Nonetheless . . . here's silver for your trouble.

CROSSING SWEEPER. God bless you, sir.

D'ORSAY. And now, if you'll excuse me, I have a rather pressing appointment with a Mr Corneilson in George Street . . . whose high artistry in the construction of picture frames . . . is matched only by his exceedingly low prices.

*He hurries away.*

### Scene One

*The Black Lamb.*

*The upstairs room of a dingy tavern situated in the Rookeries, a network of shabby tenements in the heart of London's West End.*

FRIEDRICH, *a young man, sits at one of the tables. He is absorbed in a book. A man in a shabby greatcoat,* OLD JACK, *sits at another table, smoking a clay pipe. And* MRS KETTLE, *a drunken woman in a buttoned-up dress, sits nearby, sipping the last of her gin.*

*A fiddle plays.*

CHAS VELLINS *bustles through the central doors, carrying a tray of drinks. He is a bald, middle-aged man with a heavy moustache, wearing a long apron.*

CHAS. I took the liberty of ordering you another, Mrs K.

*He serves* MRS KETTLE *with another glass of gin.*

MRS KETTLE. I hope it's a large one, Chas.

*He places a beer on* FRIEDRICH's *table and a tankard of cider in front of* OLD JACK.

LIZZIE (*from the street*). Violets! Who'll buy my sweet violets!

MRS KETTLE (*fumbling in her purse*). I'll settle up with you at the end of the night.

BETH (*from the street*). Creases! Four bunch a penny!

TOMKINS *enters the bar. He slumps down in one of the chairs.*

TOMKINS. A pint of your best bitter, Chas. Nothing stronger, I've still got work to do.

CHAS. How's trade?

TOMKINS. Fair to middlin'. Parting people from their readies these days . . . I tell you . . . it's like prising the innards out of a whelk.

CHAS. Sam!

*A small boy,* SAM, *runs in.*

Fetch me up a pint of best, would you, lad. I've been on my feet all day. I just want to sit here nice and quiet for a while and enjoy this little cigar.

SAM. Yes, sir.

*He hurries out again, as* CHAS *eases his weight into a chair.*

CHAS. Scrawny little bugger . . . Do him good to work up a bit of breeches-arse steam.

*Silence, as* LOVETT *enters the premises. He surveys the room, unsure how to conduct himself.*

Evening.

LOVETT. Good evening.

> LOVETT *is made even more uncomfortable by the fact that everyone is now staring at him.*

CHAS. Yes, sir? What can I do for you, sir?

LOVETT. A glass of ginger beer. If you'd be so kind.

> *Silence. Then* MRS KETTLE *lets out a screech of hardly suppressed laughter.*

CHAS. You're sure about that, sir?

LOVETT. I'm positive. Yes.

CHAS. The ale here is most excellently well maintained.

LOVETT. I don't drink hard liquor.

CHAS. Ale could hardly be said to be 'hard liquor', sir.

LOVETT. I don't drink beer either. Or any other spirituous substance you may care to name. I'm thirsty. That's all.

CHAS. Whatever you say, sir.

LOVETT. I haven't stopped talking since ten o'clock this morning.

CHAS. Sam!

SAM (*off*). Yes, sir?

CHAS. While you're about it, lad, can you bring me up a glass of ginger beer as well?

> SAM *reappears at the door, a half-filled glass of beer in his hand.*

SAM. Ginger *what*, sir?

CHAS. Beer. Ginger beer. Look behind the pumps, you'll find a few bottles tucked away there!

SAM. Sir.

> *He runs back down to the bar below.* LOVETT *sits at an unoccupied table.*

MRS KETTLE. A man of principle, I see.

LOVETT. Aye. Well. It's been said before. And not always as a compliment, I can assure you.

CHAS *pulls up a chair next to* TOMKINS.

CHAS (*lowered voice*). From what I can gather, there's a gentleman putting up two hundred rats at The King's Head tonight. Pitting them against a pair of his own dogs. Good-quality rats they are, too. None of your sewer vermin.

OLD JACK. A dreadful thing, your sewer rat.

CHAS. Pipe down.

FRIEDRICH *starts to laugh.*

You don't want to get him started, believe me.

FRIEDRICH. It's so funny . . .

FRIEDRICH *has a heavy German accent. He is seventeen years old, dressed in the Bohemian style.*

It's so extraordinary . . . that this, for you, is a sport . . . this fighting between dogs and rats. So ironic.

SAM *reappears, very carefully carrying a tray bearing a tankard of ale and a bottle of ginger beer.*

Surely you can see that the rats are yourselves. And the dogs are your oppressors. There are more of you, yes. But not so powerful, I think, as the class above. They have their teeth on your windpipe, my friends. You make a move and . . . (*Drawing a finger across his throat.*) Pfffft! They choke you to death.

OLD JACK. You don't allus have to lie back and offer 'em your throat, tha' knows. There's other options.

CHAS. Steady on now.

OLD JACK. Give 'em a bloody nose! That were our watchword.

CHAS *takes the tray from* SAM *and serves* LOVETT *with the ginger beer.*

LOVETT. What's that come to?

CHAS. To you, sir . . . a penny ha'penny.

*LOVETT searches his pockets and then places twopence on the table top.*

OLD JACK. We smote 'em, sirs! I'm telling you. Like Samson smote the Philistines, with his paltry jawbone . . .

CHAS. I did warn you.

OLD JACK. Laid waste the spawn of Moloch, sir! And his great Behemoths of coal and steam, fuelled by the fires of hell!

CHAS. Hey. Hey. Hey. I've told you. That's enough.

*He places the beer in front of TOMKINS, who downs it thirstily.*

OLD JACK. We broke the frames with our hammers! Ripped out pins and ratchets with our bare hands! Stuck our blades into the belly of the furnace and watched the great beast die, oozing molten metal, sirs, in a shower of burning coals!

*He drains his tankard.*

Give us another drink, Chas. I'm working up a fair thirst here.

CHAS. Now listen here, Old Jack. We'll have less of the noise, if you don't mind. I've told you countless times before. Puts the customers right off their beer.

*OLD JACK holds a finger to his lips, nodding his head in agreement. He seems cowed, and shuffles back into his seat.*

Any more of it and you're out on your ear. Understand? I'm not telling you twice.

*LIZZIE hurries into the tavern with a tray of bunched violets. Her shawl pulled up over her head. She is sixteen years old.*

Thank you very much, sir. (*He pockets the change LOVETT left on the table.*) Yes, Lizzie? What is it?

LIZZIE. I'm here to beg a favour, Mr Vellins. It's not for me – it's for my sister, Beth.

CHAS. Spit it out, girl.

LIZZIE. She's been out there since dawn, sir, on an empty stomach. And she's near to perished.

*CHAS looks out into the street. BETH, tightly wrapped in a shawl, sits slumped against a wall.*

CHAS. I suppose a little brandy and water wouldn't go amiss?

*He gets to his feet.*

I'll go have a word with the missis, see what I can do.

*He goes out.*

TOMKINS. You want to watch who you're calling a rat, my son . . . in this 'ere neck of the woods.

FRIEDRICH. Please.

TOMKINS. If you want to stay healthy, that is.

*MRS KETTLE joins LOVETT at his table. She pulls out a chair.*

MRS KETTLE. May I?

FRIEDRICH (*to* TOMKINS). Believe me. I do not under-estimate the suffering of your class.

*LOVETT gestures for her to sit down.*

In Manchester, for example . . . where my father owns a factory . . . I have witnessed things would break your heart.

*A woman, MRS HARRINGTON, can be seen in the street outside, accompanied by her servant, JENKINS. She stops in concern when she finds BETH slumped against the wall.*

MRS KETTLE. I can see you're purposeful in your habits, sir, but if you were to consider a little diversion . . . there's a premises in Seven Dials, might be to your liking.

*She smiles lewdly.*

Within spitting distance, as you might say.

*FRIEDRICH laughs, amused by LOVETT's embarrassment.*

Cream tarts, sir, are the speciality, and other delicate morsels, both chocolate *and* vanilla. As fine a place as any to fetch up in, sir, you mark my words.

LOVETT. Goodness gracious. I think I know what you're saying, and the answer's no, I'm afraid.

*By this stage the whole room is laughing at him.*

Thanks all the same.

*He moves to another table.*

FRIEDRICH (*laughing*). My friend, I must tell you . . . this is once happening to me. But for me it was not a shock . . . but a revelation . . . a new beginning to my life. This whore is one day coming up to me . . . this *Biergartennutte* [beer-garden whore] . . . and she is saying . . . *'Willst du mich ficken?'* ['Do you want to fuck me?'] In German, the verb 'to fuck' is *'ficken'*. You understand? Now I am from a very religious background. And I had never in my life heard such things before. And you know . . . it was extraordinary . . . *als ob ein Riegel in mir drin zurückgeschoben wurde.* [as if a bolt had been drawn back deep in my guts.]

*He stands up, self-dramatically drawing a hand across his abdomen.*

And from that moment my soul is *befreit*! [released!] Released to enjoy life in the way that a young man should.

*He drains his glass and then slams down a handful of change on the table top.*

Another beer!

MRS KETTLE. Too right, my dear. If it weren't for a bit of the other now and again . . . we'd none of us be here today.

FRIEDRICH. My name is Friedrich, by the way.

*He offers his hand, which LOVETT takes.*

LOVETT. Lovett. William Lovett.

*They shake hands. CHAS returns, carrying a small earthenware jug full of brandy and water.*

FRIEDRICH. I am a student, Mr Lovett. And I believe in the overthrow of society.

LOVETT. I'm more of a socialist myself.

OLD JACK *takes a rusty knife out of his pocket and lifts it high in the air.*

OLD JACK.
Our standard's red, my boys, the deepest red!
Stained in the blood of our glorious dead!

MRS HARRINGTON *enters from the street. She is holding BETH tightly in her arms. The child is grey with cold, pinched with malnutrition.*

CHAS. Oh, for Christ's sake. Give it a rest, will you.

OLD JACK *returns to his seat.*

MRS HARRINGTON. I'm taking this child home. Does anyone know where she lives?

MRS HARRINGTON *is a handsome, rather patrician woman in her early fifties. JENKINS, a squat, burly-looking man in tight-fitting clothes and a bowler hat, stands at a discreet distance, holding BETH's tray of watercress bunches.*

She'll perish if she stays out there any longer, poor little soul.

LIZZIE. I know where she lives. I'm her sister. Only she can't go back, ma'am, till she's sold more watercresses. She's got to sell more 'n half her bunches, else she'll get thrashed by our dad.

MRS HARRINGTON. We'll see about that.

CHAS. Here. Give her a sip of this. Bring the colour back to her cheeks.

*He stoops down to give BETH a drink.*

MRS HARRINGTON. Just one moment.

*She lays hands on the jug and sniffs the contents.*

Alcohol? Hardly the best remedy for a child her age.

LIZZIE. Better 'n nothing!

CHAS *reclaims the jar and helps the child take a drink. She greedily downs the contents.*

CHAS. It's not the first time, ma'am.

LIZZIE. I know it ain't the best, missis. But what can you do? When you're relying on folk's kindness just to get through the day. It ain't my fault if she's half-starved . . . without a coat to her back . . . I'm doing all I can!

MRS HARRINGTON. Yes.

BETH *finishes the drink and hands the jar back to* CHAS.

Thank you, landlord. Right. Let's get this child back to hearth and home. (*To* LIZZIE.) I think you'd better lead the way.

LIZZIE. Yes, ma'am.

LIZZIE *picks up her tray and they start to leave.*

CHAS. Sam. Why don't you give your sisters a hand? (*Winks.*) Make sure they get back alright.

SAM. Sir.

CHAS. Only I want you back here as soon as you're done. Is that clear? I'm not employing you out of the goodness of my heart.

*They set off.* SAM *racing ahead and* JENKINS *bringing up the rear, still carrying the tray of watercress bunches.*

LIZZIE. It ain't far, missis.

**Scene Two**

*The deception.*

*As the* STREET MUSICIANS *play, the chairs and tables are taken out through the side doors. At the same time, a bed is wheeled on through the central doors. The bedding is filthy;*

*little more than an assortment of rags. A man, MR BAINS, is lying in the bed, propped up on a sweat-stained bolster. His face is thin and very pale. SAM sits close by, holding his father's hand.*

MRS BAINS *peers cautiously around the edge of the door.*

MRS BAINS. He's just through there, missis.

LIZZIE's *mother,* MRS BAINS, *ushers* MRS HARRINGTON *into the room. She instantly holds a handkerchief up to her nose.*

Live here long enough and you stop worrying about the smell. It's the damp what does it. Gets into your bones.

MRS HARRINGTON *stares at the man in the bed. He lets out a long stertorous breath.*

He's beyond care, missis. Between you and me, it would be a blessing if he were to go sudden. But he's always been a contrary sort of chap. It's the same wi' livestock, missis. Some go willingly to the slaughter, others have to be dragged. (*She cries.*) I haven't lived in the city all my life. I can still remember the green fields and the stooks of corn.

MRS HARRINGTON. There, there. Never mind.

LIZZIE *and* BETH *appear in the doorway,* JENKINS *standing at a discreet distance.*

I never cease to be amazed by the tenacity of the human spirit. I am reminded of a stubborn plant, growing out of a mere crack in the wall, still managing to cling on to life, despite the absence of any apparent nourishment. Putting on a brave show of blossom in the spring, only to perish in the summer drought.

JENKINS *smiles ingratiatingly, soundlessly clapping his hands together.*

One cannot of course help *everyone*, you understand. But this should not deter one from aiding the less fortunate, whenever one happens upon them. It is one's absolute duty.

*She searches in her purse.*

I don't suppose you've made any provision for the funeral?

*She produces a golden coin.*

Here's a guinea for you.

MRS BAINS *hesitates before accepting it.*

Take it, please. I know that charity can seem very cold. And I know it's not going to solve any of your problems in the long term, but it may provide a little relief.

MRS BAINS *takes the coin.*

MRS BAINS. Thank you, missis. I can't tell you how grateful I am. What with Robert being so ill for the past few months, we've had to rely on the pittance the children bring home.

MRS HARRINGTON *starts to make her way out.*

Say thank you, Beth.

BETH. Thank you, missis.

MRS BAINS. Lizzie.

LIZZIE. Thank you, missis, you've been very kind.

MRS HARRINGTON. I have been most taken with your attitude, young lady. And your general demeanour. What would you say to a place, if I could secure one for you?

LIZZIE. 'A place'?

MRS HARRINGTON. Yes, a position as a domestic servant in my household in the north. (*To* MRS BAINS.) She would only start as a scullery maid, you understand, but in time, and with a little application, she would, I'm sure, soon find herself promoted to a significantly higher station.

MRS BAINS. What do you say, Lizzie?

LIZZIE. I'm speechless.

*She drops to her knees in front of* MRS HARRINGTON.

MRS HARRINGTON. On your feet, girl.

LIZZIE *gets up.*

Now we can look each other in the eye.

LIZZIE *takes her hand and shakes it, overcome with gratitude.*

You won't be able to start at once, I'm afraid. A member of staff will be in touch just as soon as a suitable position becomes available. And now, if you'd be so kind as to show me out?

MRS BAINS *ushers her out through the main door. The two girls following on behind. There is a moment's silence and then* MR BAINS *opens his eyes.* MRS BAINS *returns, shutting the door behind her, her finger on her lips.*

MRS BAINS. Don't you make a sound. She ain't quite gone yet. Our Lizzie's just showing her out.

MR BAINS. She fell right into it, didn't she? As neatly as any bird ever flew into a cage.

*He can hardly contain his laughter.*

Quite a performance, you've got to admit. I ought to be on the stage at Drury Lane. Mind you, the deathly pallor seems to come natural these days. How much she give you?

MRS BAINS *hesitates before answering.*

Come on. My eyes were half shut. Let's have a look.

*She shows him the coin.*

A guinea, my dear, is a very fine thing. (*Harder.*) Come on now, hand it over.

*She grudgingly obliges. He bites the coin.*

Seems like the genuine article. (*Kissing her.*) Oh my little angel . . . the blight what's been settled on our lives is lifting like a stinking cloud . . . blown away by this sudden change in our fortunes.

*He jumps out of bed, tucks his shirt into his trousers and puts on his shoes.*

MRS BAINS. Robert . . .

MR BAINS. A celebration is called for, most definitely called for. Not to the extent of squandering our newfound resources . . .

*He embraces her.*

But sufficient to provide us with a pleasant night's
entertainment down the old Black Lamb.

*She doesn't respond.*

Just a drop or two to raise the spirits, that's all, and then
we'll call in at the pie shop on our way home, so the kiddies
can stuff 'emselves senseless. Eh? Think of all that gravy
running down their little chops. Warms you to the very
cockles, don't it?

*He opens the door.*

Are you coming then?

*She doesn't reply.*

Suit yourself. I'll see you down the public bar.

*And he goes.*

## Scene Three

*The journey north.*

*As* MR BAINS *hurries out through the crowded yard, the
stage slowly transforms into the yard of a busy coaching inn:
The Bull and Mouth in Aldersgate Street.*

MR BAINS. Don't look at me like that. Like I'm something
the cat spat out.

*He faces up to a member of the audience.*

The rules you good people abide by don't apply round here.
We're so far down in the barrel . . . you think, we must be
drowning in all the muck at the bottom. But that ain't so.
We go our own sweet way.

*As he speaks,* D'ORSAY *slowly makes his way to the front
of the stage. He is accompanied by a* PORTER, *pushing a
trolley, heaped with* D'ORSAY's *luggage: a large trunk,
a leather suitcase, and an opulent carpet bag.*

You've got to live for today. That's the trick of it. Might sound harsh, but you only get by in these parts by staying light on your pins.

*Throughout this, a carriage is pulled into the yard by a couple of* STABLE HANDS.

Prison. Workhouse. What's the bloody difference? Either way you end up behind bars.

MR BAINS *pushes his way out and then spins round for one final word.*

You hear people making speeches, saying how it's all going to get much better. But what do they know, eh? They're just pissing in the wind.

*A harrassed-looking* CLERK, *clutching a sheaf of papers, comes out though one of the doors. He approaches* D'ORSAY.

CLERK. And which coach would you be going out on, sir?

D'ORSAY. I'm with Mrs Harrington's party.

*The* CLERK *thumbs through his papers.*

We're going north, I think . . . Somewhere north.

CLERK. I see. Yes. (*Waving.*) Over here, Mr Aldridge, sir! You've got company!

IRA FREDERICK ALDRIDGE *emerges from one of the side doors. He is an elegantly dressed African-American, with impeccable English. He carries a modest suitcase.*

ALDRIDGE. You're carrying an awful lot of baggage, old chap. We're only going away for the weekend.

CLERK (*to the* PORTER). You can load up now. The carriage is in the yard.

D'ORSAY. One moment.

*He searches his pockets for a tip.*

I know the baggage is excessive, Ira, but one does have a reputation to maintain.

ALDRIDGE. Goes without saying.

*LIZZIE runs out of the waiting area and approaches the*
*CLERK. Her face is scrubbed. Her hair plastered down*
*with water and held in place with a grip. SAM is close*
*behind her.*

PORTER. Can I possibly have your bag, sir?

ALDRIDGE. I'll hang on to it, if you don't mind.

LIZZIE. Please, sir, I'm looking for a lady, sir. She's taking me
up north, sir. Finding me 'a place'.

CLERK. A lady?

LIZZIE. Yes, sir. I were brought here a good while ago by one
of her servants, sir. He bought me a lemonade and told me
to wait in there.

*D'ORSAY is unable to find any change. He waves the*
*PORTER away.*

D'ORSAY. Later man . . . Later.

PORTER. Sir.

*The PORTER whistles for the STABLE HANDS to come*
*over. Throughout the following, D'ORSAY's baggage is*
*lowered into the yard, hauled through the audience and then*
*loaded on the cart.*

CLERK. Got any baggage with you?

LIZZIE. Baggage? No, sir. I ain't got none, sir. I didn't know
you had to have baggage.

CLERK. Go on. Be off with you. Stop wasting my time.

SAM. But it's God's truth, sir. Honest.

CLERK. You heard me.

*LIZZIE wanders away, dragging SAM with her.*

They look like little angels, don't they? Kids of that sort.
With their big eyes and their grubby smiling faces. But next
thing you know, they're up on your back and slitting your
throat.

MRS HARRINGTON *comes out of one of the doors and bustles her way towards* D'ORSAY. JENKINS *is in tow.*

MRS HARRINGTON. Ah . . . There you are! We've been looking for you for the past half an hour. Why are you so late?

D'ORSAY. I'm reluctant to go into the details, dear lady . . . but since my well publicised and by now . . . *infamous* loss at Mr Crockford's gaming establishment, I have been forced to lay off a number of staff. And I am at present without any form of material assistance.

MRS HARRINGTON. That's no excuse. You should have been here on time.

*She steps down into the yard and sets out towards the carriage.*

D'ORSAY. I really am most terribly sorry.

MRS HARRINGTON *descends into the yard.*

MRS HARRINGTON. Well, come on then. Get a move on. We really can't keep them waiting any longer. The company has a schedule to keep.

D'ORSAY *and* ALDRIDGE *follow her into the yard, the* CLERK *following, with* JENKINS *bringing up the rear.*

I've booked an entire carriage all the way to Bradford, so there is no question of us having to share with anyone.

ALDRIDGE. How very considerate.

MRS HARRINGTON. I am assured that my own conveyance will be waiting for us at the other end. So you can set your mind at rest. The journey will be both speedy and as comfortable as the circumstances will permit. Now where's that girl got to?

*She scans the yard.*

There's a slight addition to our party, Mr Aldridge. A young girl, from a rather deprived background. I'm finding her employment at the hall.

CLERK. One moment.

*The* CLERK *pushes his way back to the stage.*

ALDRIDGE. Very public spirited of you, ma'am.

*On seeing* LIZZIE, *the* CLERK *puts two fingers to his mouth and whistles to get her attention.*

CLERK. Over here, girl! Over here!

*LIZZIE runs to him, looking down over the edge of the stage.*

It would seem that I have misjudged you . . . slightly. Though given the inappropriate nature of your appearance, I'm sure you can understand why. You'll find the lady you were seeking in the yard. Just about to board the coach.

LIZZIE. Yes, sir. Thank you, sir.

*She turns to* SAM.

Goodbye, Sam. Look after yourself.

SAM. You too.

*A sudden blaring of horns.*

*The* COACHMAN *enters. He is a portly man, very much aware of his own importance. His* WIFE, *a fussily dressed little woman, makes a few adjustmens to his resplendent uniform and then kisses him goodbye.*

MRS HARRINGTON. In you get, the pair of you. Come on.

D'ORSAY *and* ALDRIDGE *board the coach.*

I'm so glad you were both able to accept my little invitation.

D'ORSAY. Delighted to be asked, dear lady.

*The baggage is now fully loaded into the cart. The two* STABLE HANDS *take up positions at the front of the cart – in effect, the horses.* JENKINS *climbs up onto the back and the* COACHMAN *takes his place in the driving seat.*

MRS HARRINGTON. We should arrive in plenty of time for the recital. I'm expecting hordes of people. Mainly from local society, but in view of the rarity of the event, I've extended my invitation to a good many acquaintances of an aesthetic disposition, such as your good selves.

*She leans out of the window.*

Come on, girl! Get a move on! Or we'll be going without you!

SAM. You'd best be off. You don't want to keep them waiting.

LIZZIE *kisses her brother impulsively on the cheek.*

Go on with you.

*The horns blare out again as* LIZZIE *descends to the yard and finally boards the coach. The* COACHMAN *flicks the reins. And the 'carriage' begins a slow journey through the crowd.*

*Almost immediately,* HENRY VINCENT *appears on the balcony and begins an address to the crowd below.*

## Scene Four

*Nottingham.*

VINCENT *is addressing the audience in the yard as if they were a crowd of starving Nottingham frame-knitters.* LOVETT *stands just behind him, alongside* FEARGUS O'CONNOR, *a strongly built Irishman in early middle age with something of a swagger about him.*

*A banner is unfurled above their heads, bearing the slogan:* THE PEOPLE'S CHARTER.

VINCENT. As it says in the Book of Revelation . . . 'The sun became black as sackcloth of hair and the moon became as blood.' These are dark days, brothers and sisters. Dark days indeed.

VINCENT *is in his late twenties. He is a natural orator.*

In times past, our priests would have told us that God was
punishing us for our sins. But in these 'enlightened' times,
our politicians tell us all a totally different story. We are told
that there are forces at work within our society. Iron laws,
governing our daily employment, oppressing us with an
economic system which by its very nature exploits the lives
of the many for the benefit of the few! And woe betide
anyone who attempts to interfere!

*Knowing laughter.*

We are told that there has to be a surplus of labour, so that
the work . . . the actual *work*, can be obtained at a fair
market price. But we all know what that means, don't we?
It means the lowest price possible!

*A muted cheer of support.*

But what about those who can't find any work? What about
them? Well, I'll tell you. According to the *theory*, they're
going to have to up sticks and find a job somewhere else.
(*Silence.*) But what if there isn't one . . . isn't one within a
hundred miles? What happens then? (*Silence.*) The answer
of course, is that it doesn't matter!

*By this time the 'carriage' has come to a standstill in the
middle of the yard.*

It doesn't matter if you're undernourished, if you're sick, if
you're in no position to feed your family or to bury your
dead. You're simply the inevitable result of a 'surplus in the
labour market'. That's all.

*A sigh of understanding.*

And can such sick and undernourished people expect any
kind of relief – any kind of financial support or Christian
charity – when the 'iron laws' of our industrial system are
turning you all into virtual outcasts? Well, the answer,
believe it or not, is *yes*! Yes, you can, but only if you're
willing to submit yourselves to the stigma of pauperism and
the crushing indignities of the workhouse!

*Silence.*

Sounds very harsh, doesn't it? Cruel, almost beyond belief. But it's this very system that the people with the power in this country are doing their damnedest to uphold!

*Angry shouts among the* CROWD.

So what's to be done? How can we even begin to redress the situation? I used to believe – I think a lot of us did – that it might be possible to change things *ourselves*: all of us acting together . . . for our own good . . . outside of any Government jurisdiction. But not anymore. It was a noble idea, brothers, but it just wasn't working. We were treading water, hardly going forward at all.

*He turns to the group standing behind him.*

And so a few of us got together . . . disaffected people, from many different persuasions, but bound together by this growing belief . . . this *conviction* that we have to get up off our backsides and *do* something. Show the bloody Government we mean business. Take the fight to them.

*An angry assenting response.*

We knew from the first it wasn't going to be easy. A single voice raised in protest is nothing more than 'a voice crying in the wilderness'. (*Silence.*) But a thousand, or better still a *hundred* thousand voices raised in unison . . . now that might well make a sound big enough to merit some serious attention!

*A cheer.*

And so what we've done . . . we've drawn up a series of demands. A *charter* in effect . . . drawn up by one of the men standing behind me on the platform tonight. Mr William Lovett of the London Working Men's Association.

LOVETT *shuffles modestly forward and acknowledges the cheering of the* CROWD.

And what we're demanding, brothers and sisters, are the following: Members of Parliament to be paid for their services! And no more property qualifications!

*A cheer.*

Equal electoral constituencies!

*Another cheer.*

*Yearly* parliaments! And a vote – by ballot – for every man in the country!

*He shouts above the cheers.*

Yes, this is the *charter* you've been hearing so much about, brothers and sisters! This is the charter to be laid at Parliament's door!

*He points to the banner above his head.*

For it's not until these demands of ours are put in place . . . No. I'll go further . . . not until they are firmly embedded in our constitution . . . that we can begin to build the free and the just society that we all so dearly long for. For these are our rights, brothers. Our natural rights!

*He steps down from the platform to enthusiastic applause.*

COACHMAN. We'll be lodging here in Nottingham tonight, ladies and gentlemen, at The White Lion Hotel.

*He flicks the reins and the cart sets off across the yard.*

ALDRIDGE. Who *are* these people?

COACHMAN. Weavers, sir. Frame-knitters. They're the chaps who weave your stockings for you, sir.

ALDRIDGE. Back home in America, people of my race are afforded little respect, even in the 'freedom-loving' north. And in the south of my country . . . men such as I are worn like shoes on their owner's feet. But these poor souls, with their swollen bellies and rotten teeth, are surely citizens of hell.

COACHMAN. Not enough work for 'em, sir, that's the problem.

D'ORSAY. We should be reaching down to these people, offering them our support and consolation. For only by such unselfish acts is one's true nobility revealed. And then one

day, perhaps, borne up in the arms of righteousness, they
may be able to take their place in society with a full stomach
and a grateful heart. For it is unthinkable, is it not, that they
should ever be in a position to do it for themselves.

COACHMAN. God forbid.

D'ORSAY (*to* MRS HARRINGTON). Do you think this girl
of yours might be persuaded to take a bath?

COACHMAN (*flicking his whip at the crowd*). Get back! This
is none of your riffraff here, this is your actual Lords and
Ladies of the realm.

## Scene Five

*Lovett is warned off.*

*A side door opens and* VINCENT *emerges, followed at a slight
distance by* O'CONNOR *and* LOVETT.

VINCENT. I'd better be making tracks. A mountain of
correspondence to attend to . . . before I finally turn in.

O'CONNOR. Haven't we all?

*Uneasy silence.*

VINCENT. Goodnight then, Bill. Feargus . . .

*He shakes them by the hand.*

See you at the meeting tomorrow. Ten-thirty sharp, remember.
At The Blackamoor's Head.

LOVETT. And let's all try and keep our tempers this time.

VINCENT. Yes.

LOVETT *watches him go.*

O'CONNOR. I thought you were down to speak tonight.

LOVETT. I was. Yes.

O'CONNOR *mooches about, hands thrust deep into his
pockets; bullish, restless.*

O'CONNOR. It was an opportunity missed, Mr Lovett. That audience . . . I'm telling you . . . they were there for the taking.

LOVETT. Were they really?

O'CONNOR. They would have been clay in my hands.

LOVETT. Yes. I daresay.

O'CONNOR *wanders towards the inn door and peers inside.*

I chose not to speak tonight, because it didn't seem necessary. Henry spoke very responsibly, I thought. And for a very long time.

*A stranger,* OLIVER WADHAM, *approaches, loitering in the shadows.*

It was a relief to hear such common sense, quite honestly. I mean, he does go a bit far sometimes.

O'CONNOR. Not far enough, if you ask me.

*He grins provocatively.*

You know as well as I do, Lovett . . . that we're going to have to knock a few heads together before we're done.

LOVETT. You think so?

O'CONNOR. I *know* so.

*He peers round the tavern door.*

I could do with a drink. You coming?

LOVETT *shakes his head.*

Have it your own way.

*And he goes inside. As* LOVETT *sets off back to his lodgings,* WADHAM *calls out from the shadows. He is a well-dressed, rather louche young man, with long fair hair.*

WADHAM. Good evening, Mr Lovett. You don't know me. I mean, how could you? How could you possibly pay attention to every face in the crowd? I've been attending

your meetings for quite some time. Enjoy listening to what
you've got to say. Always very lucid. Very levelheaded.
I like that.

LOVETT. Thank you.

WADHAM. And it's important to keep a level head in these
perilous times. Wouldn't you say?

LOVETT *chooses not to respond.*

I mean, it doesn't do to rush into things. Not in the present
climate. Doesn't do to be too headstrong. Too red-blooded.
Like that other chap on the platform. The Irishman,
O'Connor.

*He glances through the central doors into the inn.*

Not of the highest rank, I have to say.

*He has a habit of letting his words hang in the air. Like a
fisherman baiting a hook.*

Quite frankly, I was surprised to find you sharing the same
platform. Comes from a rather odd family. They seem to
fancy they're descended from the old Kings of Ireland.
Ridiculous really.

*He laughs.*

No. The Government's never looked kindly on those who
seek to upset the apple cart. I mean, it's all very well
demanding 'votes for all' and so forth, but there was a time
when that kind of talk could get a chap sent to the gallows.
And not so very long ago.

LOVETT. Who *are* you?

*Silence.*

WADHAM. I'm no one very special, Mr Lovett. Just a chap
with his country's best interests at heart. I suppose that's the
best way of putting it.

LOVETT. Because if you're seeking to intimidate me, you're
wasting your breath.

WADHAM. Far be it from me.

*Silence.*

No. I'm just reminding you, I suppose, that the game you're now playing is for *very* high stakes.

LOVETT. Who the hell are you?

*No response.*

How dare you suggest that I'm merely . . . 'playing games'? How dare you?

*He sets off into the night. Then thinks better of it.*

If you want the truth, I'm *merely* seeking to give the people what they have a right – a *'natural* right' – to expect. That's all.

WADHAM. The point is taken, Mr Lovett.

O'CONNOR *lurches out of the tavern, a thin young* GIRL *on his arm.*

O'CONNOR. You hungry, darlin'? (*Kisses her.*) I know I am. I'm always bloody hungry.

*The thin* GIRL *nods shyly.*

There's a hostelry down the road, serves the best roast belly of pork you ever tasted in all your life. Blackcurrant tart and custard to follow. With a bottle or two of claret to wash it all down. What do you say?

*He sweeps her away down the street. Then, pausing briefly in front of one of the side doors, they enter the restaurant.*

WADHAM. Don't be taken in, Mr Lovett. On the surface . . . yes, it's true . . . he would seem to be in love with life. But in the darkness of his heart, it's death he's besotted with. Look at his speeches. I mean, the man's forever 'wading through rivers of blood'.

*Silence.*

He was once a lawyer, Mr Lovett. Don't ever forget that. He bares his teeth and he beats his chest, but when it comes to it, he never actually oversteps the mark.

LOVETT *sets off once more.*

Just a minute. Before you go . . . I don't think I'd be telling tales out of school if I were to inform you that the Home Secretary is not unsympathetic to the cause you espouse. He just doesn't believe that these reforms of yours should happen overnight. Or with any degree of violence. That's the truth of the matter.

*Silence.*

In a word, Mr Lovett, he is a man after your own heart. And should matters arise . . . which might give you cause for concern . . . he hopes that you wouldn't hesitate in bringing the matter before him in a frank and open . . . discussion . . . at a location of mutual convenience.

*He takes a card from his pocket.*

Here's my card. If ever you want to get in touch.

LOVETT *doesn't take the card. He turns on his heel and walks away.*

## Scene Six

*The return home.*

*The decorated area at the back of the stage now becomes the façade of Harrington Hall in the West Riding of Yorkshire: the primary residence of the Harrington family.*

*A wooden staircase connects the upper level with the stage.*

*A MAID runs out onto the upper level.*

MAID. They're coming! They're coming!

BARRACLOUGH, *the butler, hurries out of the centre doors below.* WILL, *the boot boy, is just behind him.*

BARRACLOUGH. You're sure it's them?

MAID. Yes, sir. I saw the carriage turning into the drive, sir.

MRS HARRINGTON's *party disembarks from the carriage.*

BARRACLOUGH (*clapping his hands*). All right. Let's get everyone lined up.

*The* MAID *darts back into the building.*

(*To* WILL.) Come on, lad. Look sharp. They all know where to go. We went over all the details this morning.

WILL *runs back inside. Pandemonium ensues: people shouting within the building; bells ringing;* SERVANTS *running this way and that. The* MAID *races down the staircase, nervous about addressing* BARRACLOUGH *for a second time.*

MAID. Mrs Burgess says she's turning over the beds, sir.

BARRACLOUGH. The beds can wait. Kindly convey to Mrs Burgess that she's to get herself down here this instant! I'm not having a slovenly turnout. (*Accent slipping*.) If owt goes wrong, it's me who gets it in the neck, not her, tell her.

MAID (*cowed*). Sir.

MRS HARRINGTON *starts to make her way through the yard, holding* LIZZIE *firmly by the hand.* D'ORSAY *and* ALDRIDGE *are close behind, with* JENKINS (*laden with luggage*) *bringing up the rear.*

WILL (*haring back on*). Cook says you'll have to give him a couple of minutes, sir. Otherwise luncheon will get spoiled, sir.

BARRACLOUGH. I don't care. He knows what his duties are. Tell him to get a bloody move on.

WILL. Yes, sir.

BARRACLOUGH. And wipe that silly smile off your face. You're not here to smile. You're here to work.

WILL. Sir.

BARRACLOUGH. And straighten yourself up, for God's sake. There's muck all over your apron.

WILL. I couldn't help it, sir. Not wi' all t' polishin' I've had to do this morning –

BARRACLOUGH. Don't bandy words with me, you young
monkey. Any more of your lip and you're back in the gutter
where you belong!

WILL *races back to the kitchens.*

*By this time, the other* SERVANTS *have lined themselves
up across the stage. High-status servants at one end, low-
status at the other. All are now present, except for the cook,*
ELI MORGAN, *his absence indicated by a gap in the line.*

Remember to smile, everyone.

*The moment* MRS HARRINGTON *reaches the stage,*
BARRACLOUGH *takes a step forward.*

Welcome home, ma'am.

*The* WOMEN *curtsey. The* MEN *bow. Their faces are pale
and impassive, their eyes lowered; all personality
withdrawn.*

MRS HARRINGTON. Well, really . . .

ELI *joins the line. He is a tall, saturnine man, with greying
hair.*

You shouldn't have made such a fuss.

ELI (*side of mouth*). If the steak and kidney pudding is not up
to its usual standards, you all know who to blame.

BARRACLOUGH. Quiet.

WILL *shuffles into place at the end of the line.*

MRS HARRINGTON. Well, it's very nice to be back, I have to
say.

*One of the* SERVANTS *starts applauding. Others nervously
follow suit. The warmth of* MRS HARRINGTON's
*personality eases the tension a little, but the* SERVANTS
*are still witheld and uncomfortable in her presence.*

(*Privately to* BARRACLOUGH.) Where's Arthur?

BARRACLOUGH. He couldn't be here, ma'am, unfortunately.
He's showing a couple of gentlemen around the factory.

MRS HARRINGTON. I see. And will these gentlemen be
staying on for the recital?

BARRACLOUGH. No, ma'am. It is, I believe, strictly a
matter of business.

MRS HARRINGTON. Pay attention, everyone. This is Count
D'Orsay. And this is Mr Ira Aldridge – an artiste, may
I remind you, of no little distinction. They will both be
staying with us for a while. Do try and remember their
names.

*There is a buzz of interest in the two men, both dressed at
the very height of fashion.*

Kindly show them to their rooms would you, Barraclough?

BARRACLOUGH. Yes, ma'am.

*He leads* D'ORSAY *and* ALDRIDGE *through the central
doors,* JENKINS *following with the luggage.*

MRS HARRINGTON. And this is Lizzie Bains. She is to be
the new scullery maid.

*She stands behind* LIZZIE, *resting her hand protectively
on her shoulders.*

I would appreciate it if you would treat her with a little
consideration, while she familiarises herself with her duties
and comes to terms with the challenge of a very new
environment.

*The* SERVANTS *stare at* LIZZIE *frostily.*

Root out some suitable clothing would you, Mrs B?
(*Quietly.*) And make sure she's given a good bath.

MRS BURGESS, *the housekeeper, gives a curt nod of the
head and sets off briskly into the building.*

Off you go, girl. Dorothy here will show you what you have
to do.

*The other kitchen maid takes* LIZZIE *by the hand and
guides her through a side door.*

## Scene Seven

*The factory.*

*The deafening clatter of a spinning shed.*

ARTHUR HARRINGTON *appears on the upper level. He is showing two men around his factory,* THOMAS DENNISON *and* RICHARD GOODE. *They trot at his heels like a pair of jackals.*

ARTHUR (*shouting above the din*). I'm not saying 'no', mind you. Not in so many words! I wasn't born yesterday! I know you don't get something for nothing in this life.

    ARTHUR *is a portly man in his mid-fifties, with a fleshy face and thinning hair. He'd be surprised to learn that, despite his best efforts, he still speaks with a Yorkshire accent.*

DENNISON. How true.

    *He shuts the door behind them. And the racket subsides.*

ARTHUR. But what I *didn't* realise, when I asked you up here, was that your offer, when it finally came, would have so many damn strings attached.

    *He leans over the balustrade, drawing the attention of the two* MEN *to the space below.*

    This is the old warehouse I've been telling you about. I know it's a dark, ungodly place at present, but if I'm to press ahead wi' them improvements, it's definitely where I'd want to start.

DENNISON. But to do that, Mr Harrington . . . and this is the whole point of our visit . . . you'll need money. And plenty of it.

GOODE. Exactly.

ARTHUR. But, you see, I've built this factory up from nothing. I've always done things my way. And I don't want to be taking orders from folks hundreds of miles away in London. Not if I can help it.

GOODE. Let's just get one thing clear, Mr Harrington. We're not a bank.

DENNISON. Get that idea right out of your head.

GOODE. What we both are, in fact . . . are representatives of a number of London gentlemen, wealthy enough . . .

DENNISON. And public spirited enough . . .

GOODE. Yes. To offer you the considerable sums that you require . . .

DENNISON. Proportionate to the . . .

GOODE. Yes. Proportionate to the amount they are willing to invest.

ARTHUR. Well, I don't know.

> GOODE *is a sharp-featured man in his late thirties.* DENNISON *is twenty years older and a little fatter, with a chalky pink complexion brought about by a lifetime's addiction to claret and cigars.*

GOODE. The thing is, Mr Harrington . . . it isn't really possible for one man to run a business of this complexity.

DENNISON. Not these days, it isn't.

GOODE. Much as one might like to. I mean, think of all the buying and selling involved. The manufacturing . . .

DENNISON. The advertising.

GOODE. The advertising. Yes. He can't be everywhere at once. Can't have eyes in the back of his head.

DENNISON. Oh, that's very well put, Mr Goode.

GOODE. And whilst remaining firmly, yes, *firmly* in control, he has to learn to accept contributions from other more informed sources.

DENNISON. Including, of course, the chaps who are investing their savings in his venture. I mean, it goes without saying.

GOODE. Like it or lump it, Mr Harrington, it's the nature of the age we live in. Everything's changing very fast.

DENNISON. And not always for the better. If these Chartists have their way, we could be in for a very sticky time of it indeed.

GOODE. Strikes. Insurrections . . .

DENNISON. All manner of disobediences . . .

GOODE. It's not going to be easy facing up to this kind of – shall we say – *onslaught* on one's own.

DENNISON. Far better to have people behind you, backing you up in a crisis.

GOODE. Far, far better.

*Silence.*

ARTHUR. But why don't I just go to the bank? Like I've always done? Borrow just enough to get the work done in here. I mean, you can see for yourself how it's crying out for redevelopment. I could get twenty more handlooms in here, easy. Thirty, if I packed 'em all in! I know it's a bit dark at present, but if we knocked out a couple of windows up there, it'd be plenty bright enough.

*He strides around the stage.*

In time, of course, I'll put the power looms in. Just as soon as they start proving themselves reliable. I don't want to lay out all that brass and find they're conking out on me every ten minutes.

*The trapdoor opens and a* WEAVER *clambers up from the shed below. He pushes a sickly-looking* BOY *in front of him.*

WEAVER. It's this little chap, sir. He's coughing bad.

ARTHUR. Let's have a look.

*He squats down in front of the* BOY, *resting both hands on his shoulders. Looks into his eyes.*

Open your mouth.

*The* BOY *opens his mouth.* ARTHUR *looks briefly inside.*

Get him back to work. There's nowt I can do.

*The* WEAVER *helps the* BOY *down the trapdoor.*

He'll be standing before his maker ere the month's out. I've seen 'em go that way before. (*Silence.*) I'm a Godfearing man, Mr Dennison. Chapel every Sunday. Lay preacher in the summer months, when the minister takes his rest. And if I'm perfectly frank with you, it isn't their physical condition that bothers me. What worries me is the state of their *souls*. And what I'm doing by employing them here . . . what I'm *essentially* doing . . . I'm giving them the chance to sweat off their perdition before the Judgement Day. They ought to count themselves lucky.

*The sound of a castrati tenor starts to float down from above:* SIGNOR CAVELLINI *is beginning his recital.*

Come on, let's get you back to the house.

*They descend through the trapdoor.*

### Scene Eight

*The recital.*

SIGNOR CAVELLINI *is giving his recital on the upper level. The guests are mostly grouped in front of him with their backs to the audience. He finishes on an impossibly high note. The essentially provincial audience, though somewhat confounded by the performance, applauds enthusiastically.*

ALDRIDGE. As you know, I am not without experience in matters theatrical . . . but never before have I felt quite so exhilarated by a performance . . . and yet at the same time so wretchedly depressed.

D'ORSAY. An extraordinary voice. Almost painful in its intensity.

ALDRIDGE. Even more so, perhaps, when one thinks of all the sacrifice involved.

SERVANTS *mingle with the* GUESTS, *offering canapés and glasses of wine.*

D'ORSAY. Is it a choice made willingly, do you think? Or is it something decided for one at an early age, with a single cut of the barber's knife?

ALDRIDGE. I don't know. Why don't you ask?

MOLLY, *a chambermaid, races down the staircase, carrying a wine bottle. She knocks on the door stage right.*

MOLLY. Mr Barraclough! Mr Barraclough!

BARRACLOUGH (*inside*). Yes? What is it?

MOLLY. There's been a mistake, sir. Mrs Harrington says we're serving the wrong wine. She'd asked for the Château Lafite apparently, sir. And we've been giving them Graves, which she wanted kept for this evening.

BARRACLOUGH. For God's sake, girl, there's no need to get into such a fluster. Get back up there at once.

MOLLY (*running back up the stairs*). Sir!

BARRACLOUGH. Keep your hand over the label when you're pouring and no one will ever know the difference.

*He strides over to the kitchen.*

I'll have the Lafite sent up straight away!

*He knocks on the door stage left and shouts through into the kitchen.*

Lizzie! Lizzie! Are you in there?

*There is a sense of heat and energy as the door opens. Steam wafts out into the open air.*

ELI (*inside*). When I say 'pluck', girl, I mean just that – pluck! Pull out the bird's feathers. Didn't your parents teach you anything?

*LIZZIE comes to the door; hair scraped back, red in the face, her apron stained with blood and grease.*

BARRACLOUGH. Lizzie. Was it you got the wine from the cellar this morning?

LIZZIE. Yes, sir. Me and Dorothy, sir.

BARRACLOUGH. Well, you made the wrong selection
apparently. Oh yes, you did. And by failing to perform your
duties correctly, you have caused your mistress an undue
measure of agitation. Do I make myself clear?

LIZZIE. But it was Dorothy read the labels, sir.

BARRACLOUGH. Now don't start apportioning the blame
elsewhere, girl. If it's your fault you must learn to take it on
the chin. (*He turns to go.*) You can read, can't you?

LIZZIE. It's not my strongest point, sir.

BARRACLOUGH. Well, next time you're given a task of this
magnitude, make sure you are accompanied by someone
who can. Understand?

LIZZIE. But no one talks to me, sir. They all hate me, sir. They
behave as if I didn't exist half the time.

BARRACLOUGH. Which is exactly the way it should be.
While you're here, your life has no meaning other than to
serve those above you. Understand? They're the ones who
actually cut the mustard.

ARTHUR, DENNISON *and* GOODE *weave their way
through the yard.*

A word of advice. (*His voice drops. His accent thickens.*)
The same rules apply here as they do in the world outside.
There's them at the top and there's them at the bottom.
You'll do well enough if you keep your head down and
work hard. But you're never going to cross that threshold
and make summat of your life. Believe me. Never in a
month of Sundays.

GOODE *assists a tipsy* ARTHUR *up onto the stage.*

ARTHUR. I have to say, Mr Dennison . . . that the excitement
of concluding today's business . . . in a manner highly
satisfactory to both parties . . . has made a surprisingly
substantial dent . . . in my customarily cast-iron aversion . . .
to the consumption of spirituous liquors.

DENNISON. What harm is there in a little celebratory tipple?

*They unsteadily ascend the staircase.*

ARTHUR (*winks*). How was the concert?

BARRACLOUGH. Ask your wife, sir, if you want a more considered opinion.

DOROTHY *hurries down the staircase, almost colliding with* ARTHUR, DENNISON *and* GOODE *on their way up.*

DOROTHY. I'm to fetch a steak for Signor Cavellini. And half a dozen oysters. Excuse me, sir. It's what he always has after a concert apparently.

*She bustles into the kitchen, as* WILL *races down the stairs with a tray of dirty plates.*

WILL. Take a tip from me, love. Keep a smile on your face. Don't ever let on to what you're feeling inside. It's all got to seem effortless, like a duck on a pond. What no one wants to see is all the paddling that goes on underneath.

*He runs into the kitchen, almost colliding with* DOROTHY, *bearing a tray of exotic-looking canapés.*

BARRACLOUGH. Dorothy, was it you brought the wine up from the cellar this morning?

DOROTHY. Yes, sir. Me and the new girl, sir.

BARRACLOUGH. Well, since the order was not apparently carried out correctly, I think you'd better –

DOROTHY. It's not my job, sir, normally. Only we've been in such a rush.

BARRACLOUGH. Don't interrupt. I think you'd better accompany me to the wine cellar, where I can safeguard any possible error by placing two of the required bottles in your decidedly unreliable hands.

*He strides across to the door stage right. And holds it open.*

DOROTHY. But I'm supposed to take these upstairs, sir. (*Silence. To* LIZZIE.) Take these refreshments upstairs to the gallery for me, would you? The mistress said it were urgent.

LIZZIE. But I'm not dressed right.

DOROTHY. You heard me.

*She quickly hands the tray to LIZZIE, and then scurries through the door.*

(*Whisper.*) It's all her fault, sir. She's simple, sir. She can't read.

*As they go inside, SIGNOR CAVELLINI, loosened up by the wine, suddenly launches into an impromptu encore.*

*LIZZIE runs up the staircase and onto the balcony. As the encore comes to its unexpected conclusion, she hurries back down the stairs again – minus the tray – and collapses onto the bottom step, biting back tears.*

ALDRIDGE. Bravo! Bravo!

*WILL emerges from the kitchen with an empty tray.*

WILL. Terrible racket, innit? Like someone slitting a pig.

*LIZZIE bursts into tears as he races past her up the stairs. At the same moment, DOROTHY pushes her way through the stage-right door, carrying a crate of wine bottles.*

DOROTHY. Out of my way, girl. I've got to drag this damn crate upstairs.

*LIZZIE resolutely stays where she is.*

LIZZIE. No. Why should I? Why should I do you any favours? You ain't done me none. Sending me upstairs just now,  in a bloody apron and a mop cap . . . What have I ever done to you, eh? Any of you? Why've you all got it in for me? Is it because I ain't got no manners or nothing? Because I talk different? Is that why you look down on me? Like I'm something spat out by the fucking cat?

*She snatches a potato-peeler from her apron pocket and holds it in front of her like a knife.*

Where I come from, you wake up every morning in a pile of rags, surprised to find you're still alive. I got a clean bed here. And I'll tell you, I ain't giving it up without a fight.

ELI *watches through the half-open kitchen door.*

You want me out of here? Well, I'm telling you, you're going to have to kill me first!

ELI. That's enough of that.

*He seizes LIZZIE by the hair at the back of her neck and drags her through the kitchen door.*

On your knees, girl! Down on your knees and repent!

*As the door slams, the CHOIR starts singing.*


**Scene Nine**

*Confession!*

*The SERVANTS file onto the upper level and, standing in a tight group, they sing the verse of a Wesleyan hymn. The central doors open and LIZZIE comes through, wearing a simple white dress. ELI, now in sombre black, closes the door behind her.*

ELI. What's troubling you, child?

*No response.*

I sensed at the prayer meeting that all was not well. That's why I asked you to stay behind.

LIZZIE. Such a big room.

*She stands centre stage, admiring the room.*

Back home we all lived in one room. Not half as big as this one.

*Silence.*

I knew things it weren't proper for a child to know.

ELI. What sort of things?

LIZZIE. What's it got to do with you?

ELI. There's no need to be ashamed. Unburden yourself before the Lord.

*She looks up at the wall.*

LIZZIE. What's all them books? Are they your recipe books?

ELI. No, child. Holy books. Learned commentaries on the Scriptures.

LIZZIE. There's things happened in our house you wouldn't wish on a dog.

ELI. Tell me about it. Ease your soul.

LIZZIE. I told you already. It's none of your business.

ELI. Lay your sins before the Lord. Find your solace in his wounds.

LIZZIE. What sins, Mr Morgan? I never knew no different. Me, I just got on with it like everyone else. How the hell was I supposed to know any better?

ELI. Look into your heart. Listen to what your conscience tells you.

*He kneels in front of her.*

Listen for that still small voice, my child. It's the voice of Our Lord.

LIZZIE. Who are you calling a child? I was never a child. I was out selling flowers soon as I could walk. Out on the bloody street! I'll tell you, there's nothing surprises me any more. Nothing under God's heaven! 'Oh you poor little thing,' these men would say to me. 'Let me buy you a cup of tea.' But go along with them and they'd soon be singing a different tune.

*Fighting back tears.*

If one of 'em slipped his hand under my blouse, what was I supposed to do about it? Start praying for deliverance? I don't think so. Fight back and you'd end up in the river, throttled with your own garters, bobbing up on the morning tide.

*Unhealthy silence.*

Look any man in the face for long enough, and you'll see a bloody animal staring back at you, with red eyes and yellow teeth. You talk about sin . . . I don't think you know the meaning of the word. I've sinned so deep, it cuts you to the very bone. I'm nothing. All used up. Like a doll thrown in the gutter, kicked up by the horse's hooves.

*She is sobbing uncontrollably.*

There's no place for someone like me in this world.

ELI. O Father God, spare this fallen child from everlasting darkness. Bestow Thy forgiveness upon her.

*He lays his hand on her head.*

Let her soul be delivered unto Thee, O Lord. Where even now it lies invulnerable, locked in the deepest dungeon of her heart. Let it rise, O Lord, into Thy goodness. Borne ever upwards on penitential wings. And find a refuge at last in Thy torn body, mercilessly crucified on Calvary's cross! Far, far, O Lord, from Hell's abominations, where unrepentant souls are stretched in anguish on the rack of eternity, crushed beneath the hissing rocks. And drowned in liquid fire.

## Scene Ten

*Torchlight meeting.*

*Woodhouse Moor, Leeds.* O'CONNOR *is addressing a vast crowd of* WORKING MEN. *It is late in the evening. He stands on a platform, erected in the yard. The* MEN *stand at each corner, bearing torches.*

O'CONNOR. After Sheffield, there's nothing to see but ash and clinker . . . all the way into Leeds. Soot-blackened buildings. Slag. Smoke from a thousand chimneystacks, blotting out the sun's light. Wasted ground on which nothing grows. Flames from furnaces, spilling out into the

night. Mill wheels turning. Great beam engines heaving up
water from below. And underground, I see men up to their
waists in muck and slime, hacking at the coal face. Women
too, skin blackened by the dust, on hands and knees,
hauling trucks to the pit head. And children, no more than
nine or ten, slipped down passageways, too small for
grown-up men to go! You know what it reminds me of?

*A long silence.*

A painting of 'The Judgement Day' on the wall of our
church back home. And it's true, brothers and sisters. A
Day of Judgement is at hand. Indeed it is. Not the bloody
Apocalypse promised in the Book of Revelation, when the
souls of men shall be judged, but a day of our own
choosing, when the Government of this country will be
weighed in the balance. And found wanting!

*A gathering murmur of comprehension and assent.*

The man who labours in a mill has the same right to a
decent life as the man who employs him! The same goes
for the weaver. The collier. The foundry worker and the
seamstress in the sweatshop! And that's not forgetting those
of you grinding your lives away in domestic servitude,
doing all the dirty work that your employer isn't prepared
to do himself! You all have a right to food, shelter, warmth,
a living wage . . . and a bit of time off now and again.

*A roar of approval.*

I tell you, a blackamoor slave in the Americas is better
treated!

*He waits for silence.*

Now at first glance, that might seem an unpardonable
exaggeration. But just think about it for a minute. Slavery
is a loathsome institution, now outlawed here and in the
colonies. And rightly so! But at least the blackamoor is
cared for, given decent lodgings and fattened up so he's fit
for work . . . which is more than can be said for most of
you, I'll wager! Here in a supposedly free country, you're
treated like dirt under the factory owner's feet. 'Let 'em

starve! Let 'em die!' seems to be the owner's motto. 'Let
'em rot! Let 'em sweat! Let 'em freeze in the winter. Who
cares? There'll be plenty more to take their place.'

*He waits for them to quieten down.*

So what's to be done? How are we going to improve
matters?

*He holds the pause for as long as he dares.*

Well, let's face it, there's nothing a man can do on his own.
Nothing at all. Singly we are weak, it's only together that
we can become strong! And a real power in the land! So let
us unite under the blood-soaked banner! Let's hack out the
rottenness from the Houses of Parliament and shore up the
old lady with some new ideas before the whole damn
building collapses into the River Thames through the sheer
weight of its own corruption!

*Jeering laughter.*

All we're asking is a say in the way things are run in this
country. That's all. A vote for every working man in a
properly elected Government! It's not much to ask, is it?

*Silence.*

Now, William Lovett and the rest all argue that this has to
be done peaceably. Somehow or other, we have to turn our
world upside down and not get our hands dirty! We've got
to overturn centuries of oppression without as much as a dig
in the ribs or a poke in the eye. Well, you know what I say,
brothers. I say – 'Peaceably if we can, *forcibly* if we *must!*'
That's what I say. Because I can't see this lot now in power
surrendering all their privileges without putting up a bit of
a fight. I really can't.

*Isolated shouts of assent: 'Let's get the bastards!', 'Let's
give 'em hell!'*

What do you do with a bully when he threatens you?

*Shouts of 'Thump him!', 'Knock the bugger down.'*

That's right, brothers, you knock him down! And if they
come at us with sword and musket, as they will, brothers,

make no mistake . . . we've got to be ready to answer them
back! Like with like! So keep your muskets at the ready!
Lay in powder and shot! For the day of reckoning is at
hand!

*A deep baying sound as the crowd howls its approval.*

We've offered them our necks for long enough. Let's show
them our teeth this time! And if blood is to be shed, then let
it be shed. Let the streets run with it!

*A great roar of assent.*

By hook or by crook, brothers and sisters, our voice will be
heard in the land! And our grievances will be addressed!

*He steps down from the platform to tumultuous applause.*

### Scene Eleven

*On the moors.*

*WILL climbs up out of the yard and onto the stage. He then
reaches down and hauls LIZZIE up beside him.*

WILL. It's great up here, isn't it? There's just you . . . the sky
above . . . and nowt else beside.

*They sit on the edge of the stage, dangling their legs.*

In winter, sometimes, you fancy the wind's blowing right
through you.

LIZZIE. You come up here on your own?

WILL. Aye.

LIZZIE. And you don't get frightened?

WILL. There's nowt frightens me, lass. That's not to say that
I wouldn't make a run for it if a mad bull were after me.
But I don't go through life thinking there's one round every
corner. What would you say if I gave you a kiss?

LIZZIE. Is that why you brought me up here?

WILL. Well . . . yes. But it weren't the only reason.

*WILL edges a little closer, wondering if he dare put his arm around her.*

I just want to be with you . . . that's the truth of the matter, really. Spend time with you. Talk to you.

*Silence.*

It were a grand meeting last night. Pity you weren't there.

LIZZIE. I had other things to do.

WILL. So I gather. (*Edging closer.*) There must've been thousands of people. All of us crushed together. Hanging on his every word. I tell you . . . it were a bloody revelation.

*He stares up into the sky.*

Sometimes when I'm blacking boots or summat, I find I'm thinking about things. About me. About you. About what's going on in the world. Only I've never has no schooling so I can't ever get things straight in my head. Give us a kiss. Go on.

LIZZIE. No.

WILL. Anyroad . . . last night . . . as I listened to the man speak . . . all these thoughts – all these half-baked notions – suddenly came clear. Like I'd been blind and now I could see sort of thing! I mean I've allus known that the folks wi' all the brass are up on t' top of t' pile. And folks like thee and me are way down at the bottom. But what I'd allus thought was . . . that it were in t' natural way of things. And it isn't! It bloody isn't!

LIZZIE. Steady on.

WILL. Why shouldn't we have a say in what goes on? Same as them? A vote. A proper parliament, which isn't rigged in favour of them with t' property. And a candidate of us own. I mean, why bloody shouldn't we? I tell you, if he'd've told us to march on London there and then, we'd've set off wi'out a word of protest. Every man jack of us.

LIZZIE. And every woman too?

WILL. I daresay. Yes. He said we had to stand together.
Organise ourselves. Make our voice heard in the land! He
stopped short of saying we should rise up and *kill* the
bastards. But if I'm honest with you . . . that were the gist
of it.

LIZZIE. I don't hold with killing. Doesn't matter what the
grievance is. It's wrong. It says so in the Bible.

WILL. It wasn't just about blood and mayhem, there was a lot
of other stuff beside.

LIZZIE. I don't doubt it.

WILL. It might be a good idea if you came along with me next
time and found out for yourself.

LIZZIE. I'm not interested.

*He moves his hand closer to hers. When she becomes aware
of this, she moves her own hand further away.*

'Life's just a vale of tears.' That's what Mr Morgan believes.
'We have to suffer,' he says 'so we can rid ourselves of our
sin. And be ready, when the time comes, to take our place in
the Kingdom of Heaven.'

WILL. Is that what *you* believe?

LIZZIE. I don't know. I *think* so.

*Silence.*

The thing is, Will . . . I've got a decent start here. I can
make something of my life, if I knuckle down. I feel clean
now. And I don't want to mess things up.

*She starts to cry.*

And besides . . . I'm not getting the cold shoulder like I was
at first. People talk to me now. Can you believe that? I'm
*finally* getting accepted. So I don't want to get involved in
something that might make bloody criminals of us all! Do
you understand?

WILL. Yes, of course I do.

*He takes her hand.*

LIZZIE. Did I give you permission to do that?

WILL. No. I just did it.

*She thinks about pulling her hand away and then doesn't.*

I'm up from the gutter, as well you know.

LIZZIE. I don't doubt it.

WILL. Just look at them stars. Makes you feel small, doesn't it? About this big.

*He indicates an infinitesimal amount of height, between thumb and forefinger.*

LIZZIE. Speak for yourself.

*She drops down from the stage and hares out through the audience. After a moment's hesitation, WILL chases off in pursuit.*

## PART TWO

### Prelude

*Brass band marching music.*

*A small group of well-dressed* WORKING MEN *process through the yard towards the stage, bearing a huge petition,* LOVETT *at their head.*

*The central doors open and the Lord Mayor's party appears. A banner behind them reads:* LEICESTER WELCOMES THE PETITION! LOVETT *shakes hands with the* MAYOR, *and then turns to the crowd in the yard.*

LOVETT. This is the petition, brothers, that's been creating such a stir up and down the country. It bears the signatures of all the people in support of our charter. As you can see, it's already a considerable document, but when every right-thinking man has put his name to it, and it's finally laid at Parliament's door . . . I'm telling you . . . there'll be that many signatories, we're going to need a crane to lift it. And when it's finally unrolled . . . it's going to stretch all the way down Whitehall to Trafalgar Square! Aye, and beyond!

*Tumultuous applause. And they go in.*

### Scene Twelve, Part One

*Victoria and Albert.*

*Windsor Palace.*

*A royal fanfare.* PRINCESS VICTORIA *appears on the upper level. Behind her, in the shadows, are two of her* LADIES-IN-WAITING.

VICTORIA. He's not there.

*A moment's silence.*

It was suggested to me at breakfast that if I just happened to be in the vicinity of the staircase at eleven o'clock this morning, I might 'happen' to run into him.

*A* LADY-IN-WAITING *consults a watch, concealed in a locket around her neck.*

Go and see if he's dithering outside.

*The other* LADY-IN-WAITING *hurries down the staircase. By taking little steps inside her long dress, she seems to float down to the lower level.*

He may well be a little shy.

*The* LADY-IN-WAITING *opens the stage-left door.* ALBERT OF SAXE COBURG GOTHA *is revealed standing behind it. He is surrounded by other members of his family. They seem a little caught out by the sudden opening of the door. Without a word being said,* ALBERT *is pushed out through the door, which is quickly shut behind him.*

Ah, there you are. What a lovely surprise.

ALBERT. I'm sorry to be late.

*He has a heavy German accent.*

My watch is a little slow.

VICTORIA *turns and dismisses her* LADIES-IN-WAITING.

VICTORIA. Off you go.

*They slowly withdraw.*

Go on. Hop it.

ALBERT *holds up his pocket watch.*

ALBERT. These German watches.

*The* LADIES-IN-WAITING *both finally withdraw.*

I am sorry also to appear gauche before you. The formality of my life here is not making me at my most comfortable.

I am feeling as a piece on a chessboard. Pushed by an unseen hand.

*He edges towards the foot of the staircase, smiling gamely.*

Knight to Queen's pawn, perhaps.

*She acknowledges his wit with a little laugh.*

*Ich verliere jede Willenskraft. Jeden Sinn meiner selbst.* [I am losing any sense of volition. Of who I really am.]

VICTORIA. Oh, Albert.

ALBERT. Victoria.

*She runs down the staircase to about halfway.*

VICTORIA. I have so enjoyed having you as our guest here these past few days. My life has brightened up no end. To talk to you is a joy. To listen to your clever little speeches. And then to dance with you . . . as we did last night . . . *Mit dir im Walzer dahinzugleiten . . . das ist ein Gefühl ohne Worte.* [To be swept off my feet by your waltzing . . . is a feeling beyond words.]

ALBERT. *Kein Mann kann alleine Walzer tanzen. Dazu braucht es immer einen Partner.* [No man can waltz alone. A partner is always necessary.]

VICTORIA. Oh, Albert.

ALBERT. *Meine kleine Victoria.* [My little Victoria.]

*She quickly descends to the bottom of the staircase and holds out her hand.*

VICTORIA. We must remember to speak English. I am to be Queen of England after all.

ALBERT. Such an onerous responsibility.

*He very gravely takes her hand.*

(*Quietly.*) In future, we shall only speak in German when there are other people listening.

VICTORIA. Yes.

*She laughs.*

You know what I'm going to say, don't you?

ALBERT. I think so.

*Silence.*

The delicacy of the situation has been explained to me.

VICTORIA. It would make me too . . . too happy if you were
to marry me.

ALBERT. I know.

*Silence.*

It would make me happy, too.

*They embrace.*

VICTORIA. Oh, Albert . . . if I had all the world to choose
from . . . it would still be you.


## Scene Twelve, Part Two

*The Christmas Concert.*

*Music: the sound of an old pianoforte striking up with the
introduction to a song. At which point,* VICTORIA *and*
ALBERT *walk down to the front of the stage and start to sing.*

VICTORIA.
    Of all the men in all the world,
    From China to Peru.
    There's none to make my heart beat faster
    Quite so much as you.

ALBERT.
    From Athens to the Tuileries,
    Schleswig Holstein to Milan,
    They've scoured the royal families,
    To find you the right man.

VICTORIA.
> It might've been a cringing Pole,
> A Lombard or a Dane,
> Or possibly an inbred Swede
> Going quietly insane.
>
> Instead it's you, oh Albert dear,
> Prince of Saxe Coburg Gotha,
> A man of sensitivity and taste,
> Neither bounder, cad, nor rotter.

ALBERT.
> We'll soon be wed, Victoria dear,
> With children round our knee.

VICTORIA.
> We'll live in peace and warmth and love.

BOTH.
> For all eternity.

*The song ends on a high note, just a little too high perhaps for both singers, who are revealed as* MOLLY *and* JENKINS, *rehearsing for the Christmas concert.*

*The* SERVANTS *of the Harrington household can now be seen watching from the edge of the stage, laughing at the song, clapping and cheering:* ELI *watches from the doorway, a solitary figure.*

ELI. Far be it from me to put a damper on proceedings, but Mr Barraclough has asked me to remind you that there's still work to be done and a meal to be prepared.

MRS BURGESS. I'll go and have a word. (*On her way out.*) Don't worry, you'll all get a running order before Friday. Once it's been properly finalised.

*Everyone starts packing up – scraps of paper, costumes, conjuring tricks – piled into a large linen hamper.*

LIZZIE. That was wonderful, Molly. I never knew you could sing like that.

JENKINS. Well, you do now.

JENKINS *runs his hands through his hair and wipes away the burnt cork moustache.*

LIZZIE. You too, Mr Jenkins.

JENKINS. One does one's best.

MOLLY. I always wanted to have lessons, but you know how things are.

ELI. Let's get back to work, shall we?

*A grudging silence. The* SERVANTS *start to make their way out.*

You've had ample time for your rehearsal. I'm sure the concert will be a resounding success.

WILL (*muttered*). Who are you to tell folks what to do?

ELI (*cold*). I'm merely passing on Mr Barraclough's instructions. That's all.

*The* SERVANTS *all have to file past him, one by one, on their way out.* LIZZIE *and* WILL *are the last to leave.*

I don't hold with frivolities of this nature. The evening of Christ's nativity should be spent in quiet contemplation. Solemnly. In a spirit of thankfulness and reverence. It should not be made an excuse for gluttony and licentiousness. (*Quietly.*) Might I have a little word, Lizzie? In private.

*He waits for* WILL *to leave.*

You were not at the prayer meeting this week.

LIZZIE. No.

ELI. We missed you.

LIZZIE. I went out for a walk. I often do.

ELI. On your own?

LIZZIE. I was taking the evening air, that's all. It gets hot in the kitchen.

ELI. But it was dark.

LIZZIE. So what if it was? It's my own time. I can do whatever I like. I don't need you breathing down my neck all the hours God gave.

ELI. Very well. I'll come to the point. This new friend of
yours . . . Will. The ugly little monkey with the dirty
fingernails. He's unworthy of you. His energy may have a
certain rough appeal, but he's hardly a suitable companion
for a fragile soul, taking her first steps on the road to
salvation.

LIZZIE. Thank you for your consideration, Mr Morgan, but
I'm old enough to make my own friends, if you don't mind.

ELI. You are aware that intimate relations between members of
staff are not encouraged in this household?

LIZZIE. Yes. It's been pointed out to me.

ELI. It's a strict rule.

LIZZIE. I know.

ELI. And were your employer to hear of such a relationship,
I can't imagine that your sojourn here would last for very
much longer.

LIZZIE. Mrs Harrington's a good woman. It's only due to her
kindness that I'm here at all. She'd make some allowances,
I'm sure.

ELI. Not if she were to find out about your past life, in the
streets of London.

LIZZIE. *What?*

ELI. I mean, I can't see her turning a blind eye. Can you? Not
if she were confronted with such a grievous allegation.

LIZZIE. Now you listen to me a second. What I said about the
bad things I done . . . it was said in confidence. It weren't
meant for your ears. All I did . . . I laid my burden at the
feet of Jesus. Like I was told.

ELI. I didn't say I was –

LIZZIE. So it's a matter between me and Him. Right? Just
between the two. It has nothing to do with you!

ELI. I didn't say I was definitely going to tell her . . . I'm just
saying, 'if she were to find out'.

LIZZIE. Don't give me that! I mean, for pity's sake, you're the only one who knows. Ain't yer? So how else is she going to find out?

*Silence.*

ELI. All right. All right. If it was absolutely necessary, yes, I'd tell her. And yes . . . let the devil take me for saying this . . . but I'd do anything – anything at all – sooner than see you fall into casual intimacy with a mere boy, hardly worthy to lick your boots.

LIZZIE. For the first time in my life, Mr Morgan, I've got my hands on something. And you're going to have to break my fingers to make me let it go. I tell you – and it's no idle promise – I'm going to make my way in the world, whatever the bloody consequences.

ELI. Then stay on the righteous path, I beg you. Forswear the flesh. I have looked into your soul and I have seen the child inside. A vulnerable child. Pitiful in its nakedness. Bound to the rock of necessity.

*He gets hold of her.*

Let me be your guide. A dear friend, with a special place in your affections. Allow me to reach into the darkness of your heart. Pluck out wantonness and luxury. And every other sin beside. So that one day our entwined souls may flee together into the wounds of Christ. And find respite in His broken body, stretched out in agony on the everlasting cross.

*She breaks free of his grip and runs out of the door.*

## Scene Thirteen

*The prize fight.*

*Canvey Island, winter 1839.*

*There's a shout from the yard, where a prize-fighting ring is quickly assembled: four* MEN, *each holding a rope, move rapidly outwards, pushing the crowd back. Inside 'the ropes', two bare-knuckle fighters are seen slugging it out.*

*It's nearing the end of the fight. Both fighters,* BENDIGO *and* BURKE, *are exhausted. Their faces (stained brown from the pre-fight 'pickling') are swollen, bruised and bloody.*

BENDIGO. Come on. Let's have you.

> BURKE *bangs his ears and shakes his head, reminding* BENDIGO *that he's deaf, and then suddenly rushes forward, launching a flurry of punches at* BENDIGO'*s head.*

> BENDIGO *backs off, ducking the blows. There is a moment's respite as both men face each other, arms hanging loosely at their sides.*

Is that the best you can do?

> *He suddenly launches himself at* BURKE *and, grinding his fist in the other man's face, he seizes him by the head and throws him to the ground.* BURKE, *badly winded, is hauled back into his corner by his* SECONDS *as the round ends.*

> *During the course of the round, a small open-topped carriage is hauled onto the stage through the central doors. There are two men sitting inside, well wrapped up against the cold: the Home Secretary,* JOHN RUSSELL, *and* GENERAL SIR CHARLES NAPIER.

RUSSELL. Enjoying yourself?

NAPIER. As a spectacle it's hardly edifying, John. I don't doubt their courage, but I've seen it displayed to more purpose on the battlefield. And much more blood spilled beside. God knows why they do it. Perhaps they're driven to it by poverty and despair. One can only guess.

RUSSELL. There's a beast in all of us. You only have to take a seat in the Commons to be convinced of that.

> NAPIER *dutifully laughs.*

Fortunately for society's well-being, the rest of us are able to keep the damn thing chained up.

> *A muffled shout from the* CROWD. *Something on the lines of: 'Back on your feet, deaf'un . . . unless you want a bottle shoved up your arse!'*

Others not, it would appear.

*There is an angry response from the* MEN *gathered around* BURKE's *corner.*

Wadham!

WADHAM *emerges from behind the coach, slightly unsteady on his feet, holding a near-empty bottle of claret.*

WADHAM. Yes, Home Secretary?

RUSSELL. Just have a little poke around, would you? See what's going on.

WADHAM. Sir.

*He clambers down from the stage and makes his way into the crowd. One of* BURKE'S SECONDS *signals to the* REFEREE *that his man is ready to continue.*

REFEREE. Seconds out!

*Not without difficulty,* BURKE *gets to his feet and lumbers forwards. No sooner has he 'toed the line' than* BENDIGO *rushes out of his corner and fells him with a terrific blow to the head. There is a low moan from the crowd.* BURKE *lies still as his* SECOND *attempts to revive him.*

NAPIER. All over, is it?

RUSSELL. Wait and see.

NAPIER *stares intently into the crowd.*

NAPIER. Good heavens. Isn't that the Third Earl?

RUSSELL. Possibly. You may even spot a cabinet minister or two if you cast your eyes about.

NAPIER. Good Lord.

RUSSELL. They're all 'in breach of the peace', you know. Every single one of them – which would present a bit of a problem if the law was enforceable . . . which of course it isn't.

BURKE'S SECONDS *drag their fighter back into his corner.*

Any attempt to suppress the spectacle would undoubtedly drive it even further underground, and that wouldn't do at all.

*The* CROWD *are still, as* BURKE'S SECONDS *attempt to bring their man back to consciousness.*

Far better to have everything out in the open, then one can actually see what's going on, wouldn't you agree? Keep the troublemakers in one's sights. Have a quiet word now and again. And make the occasional arrest. Confrontation isn't going to get us anywhere, I mean, is it?

NAPIER. No. I suppose not.

RUSSELL. Worth bearing in mind, don't you think, when you take command next month?

NAPIER. I daresay.

RUSSELL. From what I can gather, you'll have over six thousand infantrymen at your command, deployed right across the North of England.

NAPIER. Ought to be enough.

RUSSELL. Nonetheless, you're going to have to tread very carefully.

NAPIER. So it would seem.

RUSSELL. So let's keep it cat-and-mouse shall we? No mindless show of force. And watch your step in Manchester.

*He holds his head in his hands.*

Manchester. Manchester. Manchester . . .

*A cheer from the crowd as* BURKE *at last comes to his senses.*

They're well organised in Manchester and always on the lookout to provoke a confrontation. So don't you give 'em one, whatever else you do. Back 'em into a corner and, the next thing you know, it's tales of children spitted on the soldier's bloody bayonets, and you've sparked off an uprising that would spread like wildfire right across the North of England.

BURKE *gets to his feet, and stumbles towards the line. He is almost blind and hardly able to defend himself.*

Needs a cool head and steady hand. Which is why we asked for you.

REFEREE. Seconds out.

BENDIGO *is by now aware that his opponent is virtually out on his feet. He wraps an arm around* BURKE's *neck, and steadily applying pressure to his windpipe, leads him back towards his corner, where he drops the by-now unconscious man at his* SECONDS' *feet.*

NAPIER. Before you go any further, John . . . I think I should tell you . . . that I am not unsympathetic to the Chartist cause . . .

RUSSELL. I know. I know.

NAPIER. They do have a point, you know . . . when all's said and done.

RUSSELL. They do indeed. I have no quarrel with their aspirations, Charles. None at all. It's the damage they might do in giving substance to 'em, that's what gives me the headache.

*A* DOCTOR *pushes his way through the crowd and feels for* BURKE's *pulse.*

If this damn Convention of theirs gets up a head of steam and throws its weight behind the 'physical force party' . . . and if O'Connor nails his colours to the mast finally and commits himself to an armed insurrection, I dread to think what the outcome might be. Class war. Civil war. The whole damn country blown to kingdom come. I mean, it's certainly on the cards.

BURKE'S SECONDS *throw in the sponge.*

NAPIER. Well . . . thanks for putting me in the picture.

RUSSELL. Least I could do.

NAPIER. I doubt I'll be able to deliver the knockout blow, but I may well be able to cut off the supply of air.

*The* REFEREE *raises* BENDIGO's *arm and the fight is over.*

## Scene Fourteen

*Murder!*

WILL *pushes his way through one of the side doors. His shirt
is ripped and spattered with blood. He is dragging the body of*
ELI *by the shoulders, battered almost beyond recognition.*
LIZZIE *holds the body by the feet. She too is covered in blood.*

LIZZIE. Why did you have to hit him so hard?

WILL. It's done now. So don't go on about it.

LIZZIE. There was blood everywhere.

WILL. Shut up, will yer!

LIZZIE. Blood and bits of bone.

> WILL *gets his breath for a few moments.*

WILL. Come on. Give us a hand with his body. Let's get it off
the path in case someone comes by.

*He slips his arms under* ELI's *shoulders and, gripping him
around the chest, starts to drag the body upstage towards
the central doors.*

LIZZIE. I thought you said nobody ever comes round here.

WILL. They don't usually. No. I'm just saying . . . in case!

> LIZZIE *helps him move the body.*

LIZZIE. Who'd think he could be such a weight?

WILL. Let's get him under them trees. Cover him over wi'
summat. Bury him, maybe, if the bloody ground's soft
enough.

LIZZIE. What did you have to go and kill him for?

WILL. For God's sake, woman.

*She lashes out at him.* WILL *covers up and the blows land
harmlessly on his back.*

LIZZIE. I had something going for me here. As a job it wasn't
up to much . . . I know that. But at least I had a bed of my

own . . . money in my pocket . . . a bit of respect when I
went in the shop. I could've made something of myself!
Until you went and messed it all up, you bloody idiot!

*She gets her breath.*

You only get one chance in life. Don't you see? It was like
God had spared me. And I didn't have to go the same way
as all them poor damn fools I grew up with. And now what
have I got? Nothing. I'm a hundred times worse off than
they are. No bloody future at all.

WILL. I thought he was killing you.

LIZZIE. He wasn't.

WILL. What was he doing, then?

LIZZIE. You still don't get it, do you, Will?

*He shakes his head.*

It was me he wanted. Me! He wanted *me!*

*She brushes frantically at her dress. Trying to rid it of the
earth and the bloodstains.*

On the way back from chapel I could see the hunger in his
eyes. Smell it on his breath. On his clothes. And if that was
the price I had to pay for staying on here, I was willing to
pay it.

WILL. You don't mean that.

LIZZIE. Yes I do! I've endured worse things in my life. Grow
up, Will. He were only an old man, for pity's sake. It wasn't
going to be the end of the world. I could've seen it through.

WILL *pins her down on top of* ELI's *corpse, the three
bodies muddled together.*

WILL. I followed you to the chapel because I was *jealous*! I
didn't want you walking out wi' anyone but me! I love you,
Lizzie. You're the love of my life! The only thing that
matters to me. I'd do anything sooner than see you suffer.
Anything at all.

LIZZIE. Then you're a fool. A bloody fool.

WILL. Perhaps I did know what he was doing to you. Perhaps I did.

*He kisses her.*

Perhaps that's why I hit him with the stone. And kept on hitting him until his bloody head caved in.

*Silence. He rolls off her. She stares at her hands.*

LIZZIE. It's murder, Will.

WILL. I know.

LIZZIE. You've gone and murdered him.

WILL. Steady on, lass.

*He searches for a place to dig, scraping at the ground with his hands.*

It's no use digging here. The ground's bone hard. We'd never dig deep enough.

LIZZIE. I'll get a spade.

WILL. A spade's no use, we'll need a bloody pickaxe!

LIZZIE. I could get one from the toolshed.

WILL. No. It's too near the house.

LIZZIE. I'm going back.

WILL. No! We'll never get away looking like this. We need money. Clean clothes.

*She starts to run out.*

For Christ's sake, Lizzie . . . What if someone sees you?

LIZZIE. If anyone asks me, I'll tell 'em I were sticking a pig.

*She runs out.*

WILL. Lizzie!

*He drags the body out through the central doors, pausing only to yell out suddenly:*

I love you!

## Scene Fifteen

*The tavern.*

*As* WILL *drags* ELI*'s body through the central doors, the*
STREET MUSICIANS *weave their way through the yard,*
*playing a lively jig. At the same moment,* CHAS *emerges from*
*a side door bearing a tray of drinks. He is followed by a line of*
WAITERS *carrying tables and chairs, and they set up the*
*tavern, just as they did in the second scene.*

*The* CROSSING SWEEPER *stands by the crossing.* OLD
JACK *occupies his customary seat in the tavern and*
FRIEDRICH *sits reading at the same table as before.*

*There should be a disconcerting sense of déjà vu: only this*
*time* MR BAINS *is sitting sprawled at one of the tables, very*
*drunk.*

*As the* STREET MUSICIANS *step inside the tavern, they start*
*playing a ballad.*

BALLAD SINGER.
Oh he was just a serving lad,
And she a kitchen maid,
I'll tell the tale of their young love,
And how a man was slayed.

BETH, *looking a little older, and now selling flowers,*
*wanders down the pavement outside.*

BETH. Violets! Violets! Who'll buy my sweet violets?

BALLAD SINGER.
She was from the London streets,
He from the Yorkshire Dales,
But the man who came between them,
He was from deepest Wales.

MR BAINS *gets unsteadily to his feet, lurches to the door*
*and waves his daughter over.*

The cook who came between them,
A sanctimonious man was he,
He made the girl confess her sins,
Down on her bended knee.

*BETH joins her father in the tavern. She takes off her tray,
which she carefully places on a chair, and then sits down
next to him.*

He took her to the chapel,
To join the congregation,
But going home 'twas on his mind
To commit fornication.

BETH. Daddy. I don't like this song.

*MR BAINS motions her to be quiet. He is so drunk he has
no idea that the ballad is about his own daughter.*

BALLAD SINGER.
When the boy saw what was happening,
He was filled with mighty dread,
So he hit him with a rock until . . .
The cook was lying dead.

MR BAINS. That's enough of that.

*The MUSICIANS fall silent. And then move from table to
table, silently begging for money.*

For me to part with ready money . . . first there's got to be
change in my pocket, which there ain't. And second . . . the
song what's being sung had better be about something
cheerful, which this 'n most definitely is not!

*He reaches into his daughter's tray and finds a penny
farthing, which he slams down on the table top.*

Get us a drink, would you, Chas? You can take it out of
that.

CHAS. Both of you, sir?

MR BAINS. Who are calling 'sir'? You know my name well
enough, don't you?

CHAS. Seems to 'ave slipped my mind, sir.

*MR BAINS weighs up the alternatives: he can use the
child's money to buy himself a drink, or he can order a
drink for both of them, or he can do the decent thing and
simply buy one for her.*

MR BAINS. No. Just get the girl a lemonade, would you? She's earned it. Haven't you, my little darlin'?

*He tousles her hair.*

CHAS. A lemonade – with just a tincture brandy – coming up.

*He collects* MR BAINS' *empty glass.*

Sam!

*Outside in the street,* LOVETT *is approaching the crossing.*

CROSSING SWEEPER. Sweep the crossing for you, sir?

MR BAINS. Not much for a day's work, is it?

*She shakes her head.*

(*Quietly.*) Anyone been asking any favours of you?

*She shrugs.*

Next time a man asks a special favour of you, you bring him straight to me. Understand?

*She nods.*

I'm never very far away.

LOVETT *enters the tavern.*

OLD JACK. Stand by your beds! Rule Britannia! Here comes the saviour of the working classes!

SAM *appears from below.*

CHAS. Get me a nice little bottle of lemonade, would you, Sam? And a ginger beer for Mr Lovett.

SAM. Sir.

*He runs back down the stairs.*

FRIEDRICH. Welcome back, my friend. It's good to see you again.

*They shake hands.*

I have read much of this 'Convention' of yours in the newspapers.

OLD JACK. Long live the 'People's Parliament'!

*He stands up and salutes.*

FRIEDRICH. It must be making a great weight upon the shoulders. Yes?

LOVETT. We seem to be doing an awful lot of talking just at the moment. And precious little else.

FRIEDRICH *offers him a sip of his beer, which* LOVETT *politely declines.*

MR BAINS. Why then, they must be gasbags like yourself, Mr Lovett, 'orrible old gasbags.

LOVETT. Perhaps so.

FRIEDRICH. And when, may I ask, do you intend presenting this preposterous petition of yours to the Government?

LOVETT. May the seventh.

FRIEDRICH. Such a pointless exercise, in my opinion. Like pleading with the devil for remission of sins. No, my friend, the real struggle is taking place in the proletarian heartlands of Leeds, Nottingham and Manchester . . . where a social war is about to be waged, bloody and irrevocable. Not in this much-vaunted Convention of yours – where, as this gentleman has already intimated, a bourgeoisified elite, having dined to excess on political reform, are permitted to release a remedial quantity of hot and gassy air from their badly distended guts, and out through their *Arschlöcher* [arseholes] into the already much-polluted atmosphere.

OLD JACK. Amen to that.

*He salutes and blows a raspberry.*

FRIEDRICH. This is only my opinion, you understand, which I am sure is not shared by everyone.

LOVETT *is beginning to feel like Daniel in the lions' den.*

There is no need to look so downcast, old fellow. Whatever you might decide in this gabble-house of yours, the

proletariat will eventually prevail! For the working man is
holding in his own hand the key of his deliverance.

*He takes a long drink. As he does so,* SAM *appears with
a tray, bearing glasses of ginger beer and lemonade.*

The point is, you see, that political reform – however
radical, however well-intentioned – is never going to make
the condition of their lives any better. It's only by making
their lives worse in fact, much worse . . . that we'll begin to
see the fundamental social changes that you and I both long
for.

CHAS *takes a flask out of his pocket and adds a touch of
whisky to* BETH's *lemonade.*

CHAS. This 'ere's for you, my little darlin'.

FRIEDRICH. Not so much a paradox as you think. For when
labouring men cease to be merely *verärgert* [aggravated] by
the wretched circumstances of their lives and feel
compelled to *rebellieren* [rebel] . . . this, I tell you, will be
the turning point. For it is this impulse to rebel, to subvert
and finally to overthrow the existing order that is the saving
grace of the whole class.

LOVETT. And have these ideas been gleaned from what
you've actually experienced at your father's factory, or are
they perhaps a part of some philosophical scheme of things
that you're *imposing* onto our industrialised society, finding
patterns and meanings that aren't really there?

MR BAINS. What is he talking about? The old gasbag.

LOVETT. We don't take kindly to being imposed upon in this
country, particularly when it comes to theories. On the whole
we prefer common sense. We like to look very carefully at
the evidence. Make up our own minds, and then proceed
with caution.

MRS HARRINGTON *approaches the tavern,* D'ORSAY
*and* ALDRIDGE *both tagging along.*

FRIEDRICH. Look. Here is something we can all agree about.
The German Reformation gave us religious freedom. Yes?

The French Revolution brought with it political freedom. And the English Revolution, when it comes, will at last deliver the social freedom that we all crave.

OLD JACK. We shall overturn. Overturn. Overturn.

D'ORSAY. I'll just trot along to Mr Corneilson's, see if my pictures are ready. Won't be a jiffy.

MRS HARRINGTON. Right-ho.

D'ORSAY *carries on up the road, as* MRS HARRINGTON *steps purposefully into the tavern.*

(*To* ALDRIDGE.) You wait here.

LOVETT. The ideal society, in other words?

FRIEDRICH. Yes. Of course ideal! Each man an equal, surrendering his petty selfishness and working with his fellows for the common good. Not as he is now. In isolation, seeking always to get the upper hand, but enmeshed into the fabric of a just society.

LOVETT. Like bees in a hive, perhaps.

FRIEDRICH. A most excellent analogy. Yes.

MRS HARRINGTON. I'm looking for a girl. Goes by the name of Lizzie. She fled my house in rather horrid circumstances.

BETH (*shaking her father by the shoulder*). Dad.

MRS HARRINGTON. She used to sell flowers in the street out there.

BETH. Dad.

MRS HARRINGTON. I would very much like to find her again.

LOVETT. It's a very beguiling vision, Mr Engels. A vision I once shared, by the way. But can any man be said to be truly free within so *organised* a society? Is he able to make choices? Is he able to say 'no'? Might he not be as much a slave to this new system as he was a slave to the old?

*By this time it's clear to* BETH *that her father has passed out.*

FRIEDRICH. Yes, my friend, you make a good point. For it is
    the very nature of the law, is it not, to set a limit to the
    wishes of the individual.

*He circles the table, declaiming loudly.*

'And Priests in black gowns were walking their rounds,
And binding with briars my joys and desires'

– as your poet tells us.

MRS HARRINGTON *takes a card out of her bag and
writes a message in pencil on the back.*

But this shouldn't deter us from taking the necessary action.
    Particularly when you consider the suffering presently
    endured by the labouring masses in the north of this
    country.

MRS HARRINGTON. I'm leaving my card here behind the
    bar. And should any of you learn anything in the ensuing
    weeks about the whereabouts of the girl, please get in
    touch. I've written her name on the back.

*She turns on her heel and leaves the tavern, waiting in the
doorway with ALDRIDGE for D'ORSAY's return.*

FRIEDRICH. You are like a horse at a jump, Mr Lovett. The
    next step is inevitable and yet you refuse it. Oh yes, it's
    true, we might not be wholly in the right, but let's not hold
    back because we're afraid to take the risk. (*Jumping onto
    the table.*) Life is a risk! Today I'm breathing. Tomorrow
    I may be choking my last.

CHAS. Just a minute . . .

FRIEDRICH. The people are crying out for deliverance, as the
    Israelites cried out to Moses in the days of their captivity!
    So let us rid them of their misery! Deliver them from
    squalor, exploitation, hunger and injustice . . . the attendant
    miseries of disease . . . and the promise of an early grave!

CHAS. Get down, please.

FRIEDRICH. Of course. Yes.

*He gets down.*

It would be a crime, would it not, if our fear of a new society was the very thing that prevented us from bringing it about?

D'ORSAY *appears, carrying several framed pictures, wrapped in brown paper.*

CROSSING SWEEPER. Sweep the crossing for you, sir?

### Scene Sixteen

*Kersal Moor.*

*There is a loud drum roll as two separate* GUN CREWS *run out through the central doors, each hauling a large artillery piece. It's as if a bomb has gone off in the tavern. Everyone scatters – taking tables and chairs with them – running out through the two side doors.*

*A* MILITARY BAND *plays a rousing march from the upper level. And as soon as the* GUN CREWS *reach a central position downstage, they train the two artillery pieces at the audience. An enthusiastic young* OFFICER *supervises the proceedings, standing a little to the rear.*

GUNNER. Hey, you there!

*He points to* WILL *and* LIZZIE, *sitting on the edge of the rostrum, looking out into the yard.*

WILL. Me?

GUNNER. Yes, you, you stupid little shit. You can't sit there. You're right in our line of fire.

WILL. Sorry, sir.

*He jumps down into the yard, then helps* LIZZIE *to clamber down after him.*

We didn't mean nothing by it, sir. We've just come for the meeting, sir, to listen to the speakers.

GUNNER. Then clear off down the hill with the rest of them!

WILL. Sir.

OFFICER. Stand by, chaps. Look lively. The General's party's on its way.

*The* GUN CREWS *make final adjustments to their ordnance and then fall smartly into line, facing upstage.*

LIZZIE. Let's go, Will. Let's make a run for it.

WILL. No.

LIZZIE. We're not safe. There's too many people. What if we're recognised?

WILL. We won't be. Trust me. Down there we can just mingle with the others . . . another face in the crowd.

NAPIER, *now in full dress uniform, can now be seen leading a small procession through the yard.*

We'll be a damn sight safer than we would be walking down a village street, I promise you. Come on. Follow me.

WILL *leads the way, and he and* LIZZIE *both disappear into the crowd.*

NAPIER. This way, gentlemen.

*He ascends the rostrum steps onto the stage. The group following him is made up of local* CHARTIST ORGANISERS, *soberly dressed men in black frock coats, with watch chains and stovepipe hats. They are followed at a short distance by* O'CONNOR.

I'm so glad you decided to take advantage of my offer. I'm sure you won't feel that you've wasted your time.

O'CONNOR. Your soldiers don't frighten me, General. The will of the people is an irresistible force.

NAPIER. Indeed it is, Mr O'Connor. But can the same be said of those who would lead them? One suspects not.

OFFICER. Bring the men to attention, would you, Sergeant?

SERGEANT. Sir. Squad . . . atten . . . shun!

*The* MEN *snap to attention.*

NAPIER. Put the men at their ease, would you, Captain? There's no need to overdo the formality. Gives me a headache usually.

OFFICER. Sir.

*He signals to the* SERGEANT.

SERGEANT. Stand at ease . . . Stand easy.

*The* GUN CREWS *take up more relaxed positions around the ordnance, a little self-conscious in the presence of such a high-ranking officer.*

NAPIER. A fine view from up here. I've heard it said, y' know, that we can expect over half a million people. Now that seems just a little bit optimistic to me. Forty, or even thirty thousand, would be a much more acceptable estimate.

*He waits briefly for a response from the Chartist deputation. When none is forthcoming, he continues:*

Try not to think of me as adversary. We've all got our country's interests at heart and none of us wants to see this thing get out of hand. You have every right to express your views in public, just as I have a duty to keep the peace.

*He strides over to one of the artillery pieces.*

Now this piece of ordnance here, like its fellow over there, is a twelve-pound Howitzer. Lighter and more manoeuverable than the twenty-four and the thirty-two-pounder, but without their range and explosive power.

*He opens the ammunition chest.*

The Howitzer is a short-barrelled artillery piece, designed to throw a large projectile at a high trajectory. It can fire both shells and canister rounds – stored in the ammunition chest, here – at five degrees of elevation, with a range of about a thousand yards.

GUNNER. One-thousand-and-seventy-two yards, sir, to be exact.

NAPIER. Thank you, soldier. I stand corrected.

*He takes a shell out of the ammunition box.*

You can probably imagine the effects of a shell like this one, going off in a closely packed mass of people. It makes a crater the size of your living room . . . faces burned beyond recognition . . . limbs scattered over a wide area . . . and those parts of the body close to the point of impact . . . quite literally vaporised.

*He gives the shell to* O'CONNOR, *who holds it with some trepidation.*

This kind of damage isn't ever reported in the newspapers by the way. Bad for morale. 'Killed in action' makes so much better reading.

O'CONNOR *hands the shell back.*

Thank you. Are there any questions?

*Silence.*

I think that concludes the business of the day, gentlemen. Now if you'd care to follow me to my quarters, where a cup of tea has been laid on for you.

*He returns the shell to the ammunition chest.*

Or something a little stronger if you'd prefer.

O'CONNOR. Thank you. That would be most welcome.

NAPIER. If you still have any doubts about our strength and deployment, I could always prolong the visit. There's plenty more I could show you.

O'CONNOR. No. No. A cup of tea would be a good deal preferable.

*Silence.*

Or a large brandy and soda perhaps.

NAPIER. Yes, of course.

*The* BAND *on the upper level play a brass-band fanfare, as* NAPIER *leads out the deputation through a side door. While this is happening,* SAMUEL THOMPSON, *a local*

*organiser, appears on the balcony above the yard. He is
facing the guns.*

THOMPSON. Before we proceed with the main business of
the evening, I'd like to remind you that it's in all our
interests not to let our emotions get the better of us. So let's
keep it orderly, shall we?

*He waits for the* CROWD *to settle.*

At a recent debate in the Convention, it was decided that in
the event of the Government rejecting the petition out of hand,
various ulterior measures should be implemented, such as
the withholding of all rents, rates and taxes. And the creation
of a 'sacred month' . . . in which no work of any kind is to
be undertaken, until the six points of our Charter are met.

*A few shouts of support.*

These are very drastic measures, brothers and sisters, and
our delegates are of course aware that they need very
careful consideration from the rank and file before a
decision is finally made.

*He consults his notes.*

The movement is at a crossroads, brothers and sisters. The
fate of the nation hangs in the balance. And what we don't
need at this time is any talk of dissension in our ranks.
(*Clenching his fist.*) Unity is all! And so, with this end in
view, I would like to invite Mr O'Connor onto the platform.

*He stands aside.*

Up here if you would, Feargus.

O'CONNOR *takes his place, leaning on the balustrade,
milking the applause.*

I'm sure he'll be able to enlighten you a good deal better
than what I can.

O'CONNOR. Such a sea of faces . . .

*He takes a handkerchief from his pocket to brush away his
tears.*

So many people. Row upon row. Thousands upon thousands of you. Men. Women. Yes, and children too.

*He finally gets the better of his feelings and stuffs the handkerchief back in his pocket.*

I can see a day coming, brothers and sisters, when a man won't have to pawn his suit at the end of the week to make ends meet. He'll have a home of his own. Coal to last the winter. Food for the pot. There'll be warm clothes for the children. And good strong leather shoes to wear.

NAPIER *returns in order to listen to the speech.*

Oh yes, the day is coming, brothers and sisters . . . make no mistake. I see an end to your sufferings, an end to squalor and poverty, exhaustion and disease. For a new day will dawn, when the labouring man will break the chains of his oppression and step out into the cool of the morning, a free man, ready to take his proper place in society and have a say at last in the running of his country. And on that day, brothers and sisters, the six points of our Charter will become the law of the land! The unchallenged right of every living Englishman!

*A great cheer from the* CROWD.

As much a part of our everyday lives as breathing in and breathing out.

OFFICER. Permission to range the guns, sir?

NAPIER. Steady, lad. Wait for the order.

O'CONNOR. For the will of the people is a powerful thing. And, like the tide, it sweeps all before it . . . irrepressible in its surge. And woe betide the man who dares to stand in its way.

*A roar from the* CROWD.

NAPIER. Send a message down the line. No one is to open fire, unless I give the word.

OFFICER. Sir.

*He runs out through a side door.*

O'CONNOR. Let the men of substance beware: the politicians and the soldiers, the magistrates and all the petty men of office. All those, in fact, who have hardened their hearts against the people. For they will drown in the ensuing flood, as surely as the Egyptian hordes were drowned in the Red Sea, the day they pursued Moses into the Promised Land!

*Another great roar from the* CROWD, *as the* OFFICER *returns.*

Their armies will be swept away . . . their cannon turned over in the waves, their bloated bodies scattered on the plain, picked at by the carrion birds. And their palaces, their public buildings, their prisons, their barracks, and their courts of law, will slide slowly into the flood and disappear forever, undermined by the surging tide.

*This is the moment. The* CROWD *are ready to do whatever* O'CONNOR *tells them. If he pushes them into riot and the troops open fire, the ensuing bloodshed could well trigger an uprising right across the North of England.*

Such is the fate of men who dare oppose the will of the people.

*A great cheer of affirmation.*

OFFICER. Whiff of grapeshot, sir?

NAPIER. Hold your nerve, soldier.

*Silence.*

O'CONNOR. And so let us make a solemn vow, brothers and sisters. As we stand here today, in the valley of the shadow, ringed about by the forces of our oppressors.

*Silence.*

Let us make a vow to build for the future. Remembering that with unity and with resolve, everything is possible. So that when the time comes, as it must, we can go forward and claim our rightful inheritance. And venture forth at last into the Promised Land.

*The moment has passed.*

God bless you all.

*He steps down. There is a sustained drum roll as the
artillery is hauled back through the central doors. In the
balcony above the yard,* CONVENTION DELEGATES
*start filing into the seats.*

*During* O'CONNOR*'s speech,* LIZZIE *has become
separated from* WILL. WADHAM *approaches her through
the crowd.*

WADHAM. I wonder if I might have a word.

*He takes her by the wrist and pulls her to one side.*

Don't make a scene. You'll only make matters worse.

LIZZIE. You with the police?

WADHAM. Hardly. Though I am not without connections . . .
Rather weighty connections, if you catch my drift.

LIZZIE. You've been drinking.

WADHAM. True. But that in no sense undermines my
credentials, young lady. You see . . . I think I know who
you are.

WILL *pushes his way through the crowd, accompanied by*
BLENKIRON, *a tough-looking man with a lined and
weather-beaten face.*

WILL. Lizzie! Lizzie!

WADHAM. You're a dashed attractive little filly, if you don't
mind me saying so. Be a shame to see you dancing on the
end of a rope. Don't fret, my dear, I'm not going to give the
game away. Not unless I absolutely have to. All I ask in
return is that you keep me posted from time to time about
any significant developments within the movement you
support. One doesn't get something for nothing in this life.
I mean, fair do's.

WILL. Lizzie. I've been talking to this chap. He says he's
going south. Just like we are. Says he'll give us a lift in his
'oss 'n' cart. All the way to Stoke on Trent. (*To* WADHAM.)
Who the hell are you?

WADHAM. Oliver Wadham, sir. The Right Honourable Oliver Wadham, if the truth be told. (*With a little bow.*) God save the King.

LIZZIE (*quickly*). God save the King.

> WADHAM *weighs up his options. It is in his power to have them arrested, or he can continue to play a waiting game.*

It's my intention to be going, Mr Wadham.

WADHAM. Then Godspeed, young lady. We'll meet again, I'm sure. And continue our conversation in more agreeable circumstances.

LIZZIE. I trust not. Goodbye, Mr Wadham.

> LIZZIE *pushes her way through the crowd, followed by* WILL *and* BLENKIRON.

WILL. What was all that about?

LIZZIE. Never you mind.

## Scene Seventeen

*The People's Parliament.*

*Birmingham, 5 July 1839. The Golden Lion Hotel.*

*The* DELEGATES *to the Convention are mixed in with the audience, seated at intervals along the front row of the balcony. The debate is in danger of degenerating into a brawl. At the moment the scene starts, the 'physical force' Chartist,* PETER BUSSEY, *is getting to his feet in order to interrupt a speech by* JOHN DEEGAN.

*[The convention was entirely composed of working men.* BUSSEY *is a publican from Leeds,* DEEGAN *a weaver from Lancashire.]*

BUSSEY. Oh yes. It's easy enough to say that . . . Mr Deegan, but do you really *mean* it? That's more to the point. Such mindless threats are, in my view, best uttered in the taproom downstairs.

*He sits down again.*

DEEGAN. Don't you take that tone with me.

BUSSEY. From which source, if I am not mistaken, this last one undoubtedly originated.

*Laughter from the extremist faction.*

DEEGAN. Just because I've worked in a mill all my bloody life, doesn't mean that I don't know what I'm talking about.

CHAIRMAN. Order. Order. This Convention will come to order.

BUSSEY *gets to his feet again.*

Might I remind you that we're here to discuss yesterday's near-bloody massacre, not to indulge ourselves in an orgy of name-calling and small-minded inter-factional bickering!

BUSSEY. If I might just finish, Mr Chairman . . .

CHAIRMAN. Yes, but on the condition that you cease to abuse the solemnity of this chamber and address yourself to the matter in hand.

BUSSEY. What I'm trying to say . . . is that you can make all the noises you like, you can shout yourself hoarse like Mr High-and-Mighty Feargus O'Connor himself, threatening all and sundry with God knows what . . . but unless you're prepared to put lives at risk – I'll go further, unless we are prepared to put lives at risk, unless we are prepared to get the job done whatever the consequences – then we're not going to advance the cause by as much as half a bloody inch.

*Cheers and applause from the extremist faction as he sits back down.*

DEEGAN. All right. All right. So what are you suggesting, then? That we go after them like a bunch of bloody savages? And get us-selves mown down in a fusillade of musket fire?

*Affirmative shouts from the moderates.*

We're not savages. At least not where I come from.

*Muffled laughter.*

CHAIRMAN. Gentlemen, gentlemen . . .

DEEGAN. We shouldn't take it lying down. That's all I'm
saying. We should try and bloody stand up to them.

*More laughter, as* DEEGAN *sits down in some disarray.*

CHAIRMAN. For the last time, gentlemen, this Convention
will come to order!

ROBERT LOWERY, *a tailor from Newcastle, gets to his
feet, raising an arm.*

LOWERY. Mr Chairman . . . I'd just like to take up the point
raised by the delegate from Hyde.

*The* CHAIRMAN *waves him to continue.*

The action taken by the magistrates yesterday, in putting
down our meeting in the Bull Ring – a meeting which was
perfectly orderly, by the way, perfectly peaceful, until they
stuck their noses in – was a ruthless and unnecessary act of
repression . . . which merits a positive response from us.
I repeat . . . positive.

*Applause from the moderate section.*

But we can't very well march down the street to trumpet
and drum, brandishing our muskets and demand the return
of the man they've arrested, without bringing this thing to
a bloody and unnecessary crisis. Such an act would amount
to a declaration of war. A war, which at this moment in
time, we could not possibly win!

*Cries of 'Shame!' 'Coward!' echo across the yard.*

But that's not to say that we should do nothing. Or that we
should simply 'turn the other cheek', as some of the more
timid among us would have us do.

*Derisive jeers from the 'moral force' section.*

CHAIRMAN. Order. Order. I will have order!

LOWERY. What I'm suggesting is that we deal with the
Government on their own terms. What they fear above all

else is a civil rebellion. A class war spreading like wildfire
through the entire country. Well, let's play on that fear. Let's
use the threat of insurrection as a lever to get our own way.

*Silence as the point sinks in.*

If you think of it as a card game . . . we've got all the good
cards. And what's more, they *know* we've got the good
cards. This ought to be enough, surely, to force their hand.

BUSSEY (*on his feet again*). What are you talking about?
These are men, don't forget, who stake the family fortune
at Crockford's most nights of the bloody week – they'd face
you down without batting a bloody eyelid.

*Derisive laughter from the extremist faction.*

If you think you can play the Government at their own
game, you've got another think coming. (*Clenched fist.*) It's
force. It's steel. It's the shedding of blood. That's what's
going to bring them to their senses. All this sabre-rattling
isn't going to get us anywhere. Either we mean it or we
don't.

LOWERY. If the delegate from Bradford would only *listen* . . .
he'd realise that what I'm suggesting is that we try and steer
a course through that very contradiction. In other words, we
find a political solution to our present problems, which were
he not such a man of blood, he might be able to recognise.

BUSSEY. If the 'honourable' delegate feels like that, why
doesn't he own up to what he really is – a moral-force
milksop – and join up with Lovett and his bleating cronies
over there.

JOHN WOLSTENHOME, *a file-maker from Sheffield, gets
to his feet.*

WOLSTENHOME. Ah yes. But would we have him, that's the
thing?

*Laughter.*

Would such a scheming rogue be welcomed by those of us
committed to a moral solution and the peaceful resolution
of our aims? I think not.

LOVETT *stands up, clutching a sheaf of papers*.

CHAIRMAN. The chair recognises William Lovett.

BUSSEY. Holding a 'moderate' position is never easy. It's like sitting on the fence. There's always the possibility of falling off either side.

*Laughter.*

LOVETT. Fellow delegates . . .

*He waits for silence. Cold as ice.*

I think we should address the problems that confront us now, and not allow the debate to widen into a discussion on policy, with the attendant risk of becoming bogged down in the acrimony of old antagonisms. This is clearly a time for unity, fellow delegates. And with this end in view, I have prepared a series of resolutions, intended to clarify our response to yesterday's most lamentable events.

*He waves the paper.*

Firstly, that we condemn the action by the authorities here in Birmingham as an outrage, committed by an unconstitutional force brought up from London.

*A rumble of support from all factions.*

Secondly, that it's the people of Birmingham who are the chief victims of this injustice and the best placed to seek redress. And finally, that we believe the arrest of Dr Taylor offers convincing proof of the absence of justice here in England, and shows that there is no security of life, liberty or property until the people have some control over the law they are called upon to obey.

*Enthusiastic applause.*

I am also proposing that there should only be two signatories to this document . . . my own and that of Mr Collins, who assisted me in drawing it up.

*In the ensuing silence, BUSSEY gets to his feet.*

BUSSEY. You present us with something of a conundrum, Mr Lovett. Is this an act of supreme egotism on your part?

Or is it perhaps a noble attempt to draw the enemy's fire, and protect the Convention from the wrath of the authorities? Should they decide to move against us over this issue . . . as they undoubtedly will?

LOVETT. Think what you like. There are more copies should anyone wish to peruse the document in more detail.

CHAIRMAN. Is that all, Mr Lovett?

LOVETT *nods, stepping back from his position at the balustrade.*

Do I hear any voices raised against the acceptance of this resolution?

*Silence.*

Then I duly declare the resolution carried unanimously.


## Scene Eighteen

*On the road.*

*The sound of a cart coming off the road: splintering wood, the frightened whinnying of a horse.*

LIZZIE *climbs up onto the stage as if she's climbing out of a ditch. She turns and offers* BLENKIRON *her hand, hauling the old man up beside her. He grimaces with pain.*

LIZZIE. Are you hurt?

BLENKIRON. I took a bit of a knock when we came off the road. But it's nowt to get concerned about.

*He stands slowly upright.*

There. You see. Not too much damage done.

WILL (*from the yard*). I've had a look under your cart, Mr Blenkiron. The axle's at right angles. You're going to need a wheelwright, I'm afraid . . . bang it into shape for you.

BLENKIRON. The 'oss took fright. They do that sometimes and there's never any understanding why. A fly or summat

sets 'em off . . . and the next thing you know you're arse
uppards in a ditch, wi' your goods and chattels strewn out
all over t' bloody road.

LIZZIE. Shall we go get some help?

BLENKIRON. Nay, lass. You'd best be getting on wi' your
journey. Don't worry about me.

WILL. I'll get our things.

*He returns to the broken cart.*

BLENKIRON. Is it Stoke you're bound for?

LIZZIE. We're on our way south, mister. And if Stoke is south
of here, then it's Stoke we're bound for.

BLENKIRON. Right then . . .

*He looks into the far distance.*

If you want to save yourself a few miles, you can take a
turn off the main road yonder. Just by the farmhouse. See?
(*Points.*) Keep on going up yon hill. And from the top
you'll get a good view of the canal. Then all you have to
do is drop down on t' other side and follow the towpath
right the way into town.

LIZZIE. I see. Thank you.

*The old man sits on the edge of the stage, beckoning her
closer.*

BLENKIRON. Could you do us a favour, lass, and take a
message for me? It's a matter of some considerable urgency.

LIZZIE. Whatever I can do to help.

BLENKIRON. I'd do it myself . . . only the rate I'm going it
might take me a week to get there.

LIZZIE. It's all right. I understand.

BLENKIRON. It's a message from our committee in Manchester
to the one in Stoke. Do you think you can manage that?

LIZZIE. I can try.

BLENKIRON. Good lass. (*Lowers his voice.*) There's folk in
our movement beginning to lose patience, miss. They've
had enough of talking. They want summat done. And if that
means cracking a few heads, then by God they're ready to
do it.

LIZZIE. I understand.

BLENKIRON. How good's your memory? I ask because
nothing's ever written down. (*Taps head.*) It's all to be kept
up here.

LIZZIE. Right.

BLENKIRON. Once you get into town . . . make your way to
The Red Lion Tavern. You can't miss it, really. It's just off
the Market Square. And once you're there, ask for Mr Kelly.
Say it's me that's sent you. And tell him: 'Manchester's
going for the fourth.'

LIZZIE. 'Going for the fourth.'

BLENKIRON. 'The fourth.' That's right. That's all you have
to remember. He'll understand the significance, even if you
don't. The less you know the better.

WILL *returns, a leather kit bag on his shoulder.*

You can't trust no one these days. There's spies and turncoats
at every street corner.

LIZZIE. I won't let you down.

BLENKIRON. I don't doubt it, lass. That's why I asked you.

WILL. Thanks for the ride, mister.

BLENKIRON. Get on with you. Your lass knows the way to
go. I've explained her the route.

WILL (*shaking his hand*). Thanks.

LIZZIE. Sure you're going to be all right?

BLENKIRON. Don't worry on my account, lass. I'll sort it
out. It won't be the first time.

LIZZIE. Goodbye, then.

*She kisses him on the cheek.*

BLENKIRON. Goodbye, miss. Let's hope for better days, eh, when every man is given his due respect. Aye, and every woman too.

LIZZIE *and* WILL *descend into the yard.*

### Scene Nineteen

*Mr and Mrs Lovett.*

*A small expanse of yard inside Warwick Gaol.*

*A loud, rumbling, intimidating noise, as the* PRISONERS *vent their fury by clattering metal bars, banging tin plates and shouting out their anger and frustration.*

*A* PRISON GUARD *makes his way to the central doors and opens them, revealing a crowd of* PRISONERS.

GUARD. Time you lot saw a bit of sunshine. Come on. Look lively.

*The* PRISONERS *start to shuffle out through the door, blinking in the sunshine.*

Special dispensation from the Governor.

CONVICT. It's bloody freezing.

GUARD. Show a bit of gratitude, can't you? It's a damn sight warmer out here than it is inside.

*Hands in pockets, collars turned up, woollen scarves wrapped around their heads, the* PRISONERS *trudge round the stage in a large circle.*

Come on, then. Let's have walking round in an orderly fashion. And no talking.

*A solitary* PRISONER *can be heard singing in his cell: a reprise of the ballad sung in Scene Fifteen, but with a new verse added.*

Keep moving there. No talking, I said.

PRISONER.
 And where she's got to no one knows.
 She's hunted night and day.
 The coppers vow to track her down,
 And for her crime she'll pay.

 *Throughout the singing* SAUNDERS, *a second guard,*
 *pushes his way through the yard. Accompanying him is*
 LOVETT's *wife,* MARY, *carrying a basket full of food. He*
 *instructs* MARY *to wait in the yard, ascends to the stage*
 *and shows a document to the guard.*

GUARD. Very well, sir.

 *He blows his whistle and the* PRISONERS *stumble to a halt.*

 Everyone with the exception of Mr Lovett . . . get back
 inside.

 *The* PRISONERS *shuffle off through the central doors.*

CONVICT. Who's a lucky boy, then?

GUARD. Quiet, I said!

 LOVETT *is left on his own. He looks ill and undernourished.*

 This way, Lovett. You have a visitor.

 *He guides* LOVETT *towards the central rostrum, where*
 MARY *is now waiting.*

 Your charge now, Mr Saunders.

 *The* GUARD *spins on his heel and ushers the last*
 PRISONER *out through the central doors, shutting it firmly*
 *behind them.*

MARY. How are you keeping?

LOVETT. Fair to middlin'. You?

MARY. I'm not so bad. All things considered.

 LOVETT *takes an involuntary step towards his wife.*
 SAUNDERS *gives a little cough. He is not to get too close.*

 I hear you've been on short commons.

LOVETT. Aye, bread and water's about all I can stomach.

MARY. I've brought you some of the things you like. Apple
pie and what have you. Thought it might buck you up a bit.

LOVETT. Thank you.

MARY. I'm not allowed to give it you. I'll have to hand it over
to the guard.

LOVETT. I know.

MARY. But he's promised to pass the contents on. Once he's
had a rummage through.

LOVETT. Knowing your cooking, love . . . there'll be nowt
left by the time it gets to me.

*He tries to smile.*

I haven't been allowed a visitor up to now. Things are
looking up.

MARY. There's no need to act so surprised. There's some
people been working very hard on your behalf.

LOVETT. So they tell me.

*MARY grins suddenly.*

MARY. I came by train.

LOVETT. You never.

MARY. Part of the way anyway. As far as Birmingham. We
were going that fast it give me palpitations.

LOVETT. That's modern life for you.

*Silence.*

Are you managing all right?

MARY. I've had a bit of money from the Mutual, which helps
make ends meet. And the neighbours have been very kind.

*Uneasy silence. LOVETT correctly suspects that things are
much tougher for his wife than she is letting on.*

I thought you spoke wonderfully well at your trial.

LOVETT. Did I? It seems so long ago.

MARY. You stood up to them. They didn't like that. You said all those things that we've all of us *wanted* to say, but could never find the words.

LOVETT. Didn't make a blind bit of difference though, did it?

MARY. Don't be so hard on yourself.

*Silence.*

I still can't fathom it. How can you be guilty of seditious libel when all you did was put your name to a document? I mean, the whole assembly supported you, didn't they? So why are you the guilty one? And not all the rest?

LOVETT. They wanted to make an example of me. That's the truth of it.

MARY. I suppose.

LOVETT. Any news?

*She looks round edgily towards SAUNDERS, who gives nothing away.*

Is Feargus still making those damnfool speeches?

MARY. He's out of the country. Ireland somewhere. People are saying he's run away.

LOVETT. I'm not surprised. He never did have much stomach for a fight.

MARY. He's not been well. That's what they say anyway. It's his nerves, apparently.

SAUNDERS. Time's nearly up, missis.

LOVETT (*quickly*). What's become of the Convention? Has it been wound up finally? Has everyone gone home?

MARY. It's all over. No one's interested in talking anymore. They want to be up and doing.

SAUNDERS. Let's be having you.

*He gets to his feet in order to show MARY out.*

MARY (*quickly*). It was the size of the vote in Parliament. That's what did it. Knocked the stuffing out of everyone. Only forty-six votes for the Charter. Nearly two-hundred-and-fifty against.

*She gives the basket to* SAUNDERS, *who blows his whistle and the* GUARD *comes marching out through the central doors in order to escort* LOVETT *back into the prison.*

(*Quietly.*) There's talk of war. There's talk of insurrection. But it's not in the open anymore. It's all going underground.

LOVETT. Goodbye, Mary love. Thanks for making the effort.

MARY. Goodbye, love.

*In the confusion of the departure she kisses him quickly on the cheek.*

SAUNDERS. Now then.

LOVETT *is marched back into the prison.*

*The sound of a ramshackle* MARCHING BAND, *playing in the yard outside the theatre.*

*As* SAUNDERS *escorts* MARY *through the yard, he surreptitiously breaks off a slice of apple pie and shoves it greedily into his mouth.*

## Scene Twenty

*The message.*

*A hillside above the Ebbw river, near Risca in Wales. WILL climbs up onto the stage, the kit bag on his shoulder.*

WILL. Not far now.

LIZZIE. You're sure of that, are you?

WILL. Follow the river south. That's what they told us back in the village.

LIZZIE. I'm surprised you knew what they were talking about. Stupid bloody Welsh bastards.

*Close to exhaustion, she struggles up onto the stage.*

Talking behind your back half the time. Why can't they speak proper English?

WILL. You've not forgotten the message.

LIZZIE. Don't go on about it, for pity's sake.

WILL. It's important, this one.

LIZZIE. I know.

WILL. The most important message so far.

LIZZIE. Stop worrying, will you? It's all up here. (*Taps head.*) Safely stowed away.

WILL. Good.

LIZZIE. What's that supposed to mean? 'Good'? What are you going on at me for?

WILL. I'm not.

LIZZIE. Have I let anyone down so far?

WILL. No.

LIZZIE. Do you want me to say it to you, eh? Prove I still know it?

WILL. No. Not if you're sure. (*Silence.*) I trust you.

LIZZIE. Oh, do you? Do you really?

WILL. Yeah. I do.

*She sits down on the grass.*

LIZZIE. Anyway . . . I'm hungry.

WILL. There's an apple left over from this morning, I think, but nowt much else.

LIZZIE. That'll do. Eh?

*He gets an apple out of the kit bag and cuts it in half.*

(*Going over the message.*) 'To John Frost and Zepheniah Williams. Should you succeed in your objective, delay the mailcoach out of Newport. Its failure to arrive in Birmingham on the fourth of this month will be taken as a sign of your success. And light the flame of insurrection the length and breadth of the land.'

*Silence.*

See. I *do* know it.

WILL. Have a bit of apple and shut up.

*They eat.*

Clever idea, that.

LIZZIE. What?

WILL. The idea of something *not* happening being the signal. Very clever.

LIZZIE. Too clever, if you ask me. Is there any of that water left?

WILL. Sorry.

*She bursts into tears.*

What's the matter? (*Putting an arm around her shoulder.*) You're tired, love. That's all. You've made such an effort . . . getting us here. It's worn you out.

LIZZIE (*sobbing*). But it's all my fault!

WILL. Lizzie.

LIZZIE. Well, it is. If it wasn't for me, we wouldn't be in this bloody mess, would we?

WILL. Don't talk daft.

LIZZIE. Eli was always saying life was a penance. Maybe he was right.

WILL. Don't start that again. I'm the guilty one. Me! I did the damage.

LIZZIE. You don't know the half of it. If I'd never let a man touch me, perhaps it wouldn't've come to this.

WILL. For God's sake, Lizzie.

LIZZIE. I should've slapped his face for him, the canting
bloody hypocrite . . . and taken the consequences.

WILL. Why do we argue so much? It were never like this
when we started out.

LIZZIE. Sometimes, when we're on the road, I think I hear
these footsteps behind me. And I turn round like I'm half
expecting a tap on my shoulder. But it's only you, dogging
at my heels, like the shadow of my sin.

WILL. It's starting to rain.

*Music. A* MARCHING BAND *playing in the distance.*
*Rowdy singing.*

LIZZIE. What's that noise?

WILL *runs to the front of the stage and stares out over the*
*heads of the audience.*

WILL. There's people down there. See them? There through
the trees.

LIZZIE *joins him.*

A whole mass of people, marching down the valley. Singing
their bloody hearts out.

### Scene Twenty-One

*Newport.*

*The* BAND *enters the yard, beating out a wild marching*
*rhythm. They should be imagined as heading a column of*
*armed miners, perhaps as many as five thousand strong.*
*Throughout the early part of the scene, the* LEADERS *slowly*
*push their way through the crowd, getting as close to the stage*
*as they can.* WILL *and* LIZZIE *are both a little way behind,*
*clutching makeshift weapons.*

*On the balcony above the stage,* SPECIAL CONSTABLE
HATTERSLY *is viewing the approach of the mob through*
*a telescope. A soldier,* LIEUTENANT GRAY, *stands at his*

*side.* MAYOR JOHN PHILLIPS *hurries out to join them. He is
a well-dressed, rather portly man in his early fifties.*

PHILLIPS. How many do they number?

HATTERSLY. Hard to say, sir. The front of the column's just
turning into Commercial Street, sir . . . while the stragglers
are still stretched out up the valley.

PHILLIPS. Thousands, would you say?

HATTERSLY. Thousands, sir. Most definitely.

PHILLIPS. Do they look like they mean business?

HATTERSLY. Well, they certainly don't look like they're out
there picking blackberries, sir.

*A* WOMAN's *voice rings out from the yard.*

WELSH WOMAN. *Rho 'n dynion ni yn ol y diawled, neu mi
dora ni gwd pob un ohonno chi yn ddarnau a'i bwydo nw
i'r llygod mawr!* [Give us our men back, you bastards, or
we'll scythe off your bloody bollocks and feed them to the
rats!]

PHILLIPS. I think you'd better get down there, Hattersly. Get
the boys organised into some sort of a line.

HATTERSLY. I can't see them being overly enthusiastic, but
I'll see what I can do.

LIEUTENANT GRAY. Mr Phillips.

PHILLIPS. We had over sixty Specials sworn in last week,
which ought to be sufficient to our needs.

LIEUTENANT GRAY. Mr Phillips. If I might get a word in
edgeways.

HATTERSLY *leaves the upper level through the rear exit
and, using the internal staircase, descends to the stage.*

PHILLIPS. One moment, Lieutenant. And make sure they are
all issued with a bludgeon of some kind! I'm sorry,
Lieutenant, you were saying?

LIEUTENANT GRAY. Deploying your chaps down there. Not
a good idea, sir. Impedes our line of fire.

PHILLIPS. I'm doing my best, damn it.

LIEUTENANT GRAY. Don't want to be shootin' at our own side.

PHILLIPS. What I'm hoping, Lieutenant, is that there won't be any shooting. May I remind you that I am a surgeon by profession, not a bloody soldier, and if I see a way of sorting this thing out in a civilised fashion, I'm damned well going to take it.

HATTERSLY *comes running out of the door below.*

HATTERSLY. Sir! Sir!

PHILLIPS. I don't want dead men on my conscience. Yes, Hattersly? What is it?

HATTERSLY. The boys are very reticent, sir. I find myself unable to coax any of them out.

PHILLIPS. Get back in there, man, and put the bloody fear of God into them!

HATTERSLY (*running back inside*). Sir.

PHILLIPS. I want them out on the streets while there's still time!

WELSH WOMAN. *Ildia'r carcharorion! Wyt ti'n clywed Meistr Phillips? Neu mi blinga'i di'n fyw a mi hyngiai dy gorff llwm o'r polyn baner.* [Surrender your prisoners! Do you hear me, Mr Phillips? Or we'll flay you alive and hang your bloody hide from the flagpole.]

PHILLIPS. If the worst comes to the worst, Lieutenant – and I'm saying if, *if* our worst fears were to be realised – would your men open fire? (*Before he can reply.*) I ask because there's a feeling in the valleys that they *wouldn't* . . . that Welshmen *wouldn't* open fire on Welshmen, whatever the provocation.

LIEUTENANT GRAY. This lot would shoot their own mothers, sir, if I gave them the order.

HATTERSLY *comes running out of the door.*

HATTERSLY. Sir! Sir! It's no good, sir. There's most of them got friends and family out there with the marchers, sir. You'd need dynamite to shift them.

PHILLIPS. But they were sworn in. God damn it.

HATTERSLY. Yes, sir.

*A cheer from the* CROWD *as the two leaders of the march,* JOHN FROST *and* ZEPHANIAH WILLIAMS, *climb the rostrum steps.*

PHILLIPS (*a tantrum*). Don't they understand, Hattersly, that if we acquiesce to the rioters' demands, our world will be thrown into the direst chaos, spinning topsy-turvey like washing in a laundry tub, with the scum rising to the top?

WILLIAMS. I trust that last remark wasn't directed at me, John Phillips.

HATTERSLY. I'm going back inside, sir. I'm not staying out here like the sacrificial lamb.

*Jeering laughter as he runs back inside the building.*

WILLIAMS. What we are here for, John – as you know full well – is to obtain the release of our comrade, Henry Vincent. Oh yes, and while you're at it, you might do well to release the men you picked up this morning. On the steps of this very hotel, I believe.

PHILLIPS. Deploy the men, Lieutenant. As you see fit.

LIEUTENANT GRAY *hurries out through the back.*

WILLIAMS. What we dispute, John, is that these gentlemen have done anything wrong, when what they are fighting for is the basic and undeniable right of every man and woman in this country. How, we ask, in the name of all that's reasonable, can this be interpreted as an act of treason? Such men, in our view, should be given a public service medal . . .

*Laughter.*

. . . and not thrown into the deepest dungeons of the land.

*He waits for silence.*

A word of warning, John. I'm not here to cause trouble.
As you well know, I am a man of property, with money in
my pocket. And a steadfast believer in the power of reason
and the use of moral force. But I am only one voice among
many. There's men behind me, John, been tramping over
hill and dale since yesterday morning, through mud and
driving rain and without any proper sustenance. Men so
oppressed, so desperate, they'd stop at nothing to satisfy
their overwhelmingly just demands.

WELSH WOMAN. *Dyna ni beth dych chi'n ddisgwyl
amdano? Y cociau wyn! Y cachgwn rhacs! Ewch mewn i
fana!* [That's right! What are you waiting for? You ragged-
arsed, lily-livered bunch of cowards! Get in there!]

*A group of* MEN (WILL *among them*) *scramble up onto the
stage and force their way through the stage-left door.*

WILLIAMS. There's a tide at our backs, John, pushing us
irresistibly forward. And when it breaks over us, I'm telling
you, there'll be not a man left alive, nor a building left
standing!

*As he speaks,* LIZZIE *and the* WELSH WOMAN *climb up
onto the stage.*

*A drum roll from the snare drummers in the* BAND *and the
central doors are thrown open, revealing a solid rank of*
RED COATS (*the front row kneeling, the second row
standing*) *muskets pointed towards the audience.*

LIEUTENANT GRAY. Front rank . . . Take aim . . .

FROST *and* WILLIAMS *hurriedly take cover, retreating
down the rostrum steps and mingling with the crowd.*

Fire!

*A loud volley from the muskets. The group climbing onto the
stage are caught in the line of fire.* LIZZIE *drops down,
fearing another volley.*

Second rank . . .

*The front rank, having fired the first volley from a kneeling position, now retreat behind the second rank, in order to reload.*

Target . . . right. Ninety degrees . . .

*The muskets swing round through ninety degrees.*

Fire!

*A second volley is fired, not towards the crowd this time, but sideways into the building. The stage-right door bursts open and one of the attackers falls dead onto the stage. WILL then lurches through the door behind him and collapses on the floor, a musket ball lodged in his leg.*

WILL. Over here, girl. Out of their line of fire. Quick! Before they shoot again.

*LIZZIE runs to him.*

LIZZIE. You're hurt.

WILL. Don't touch . . . Got to keep a tight grip . . . Losing too much blood.

LIZZIE. Can you walk?

*He tries to get to his feet.*

Lean on me. Come on. I can take your weight.

WILL. What's the point, Liz? Be honest. I'm not going anywhere. Not with a musket ball smashed through my legbone. I'm dead meat.

LIZZIE. No! We've come this far together. We'll see it through together . . . like we've always done. Make a bloody effort! Come on!

WILL. Just hold on a minute. Let me get my breath.

*He drops back down again.*

God only knows . . . I'm grateful you've stuck by me this far. But you'd be a fool to stick by me any longer. I'm going down.

LIZZIE. Don't talk like that!

WILL. I'm going down, Liz! There's no two ways about it. What's the point dragging you down with me? So get off now . . . eh? While you've got the chance. Make a new start in life.

LIZZIE. I can't, Will. It just doesn't seem right.

WILL. Listen, lass. They needn't know you were ever there. No, listen. When they ask me, 'Was she there with you?' I'll tell 'em nowt.

*PHILLIPS comes out of the central doors. He holds a handkerchief to his badly bloodstained face as he picks his way through the bodies in the yard.*

LIZZIE. But it was *my* fault!

WILL. Don't start that – I'm the guilty one. Me! You can't go on blaming yourself. You were nowt but an accessory. (*Overriding her objections.*) I'm telling you. I'm *telling* you, Lizzie. Keep me company over the next few weeks and they'll hang *you* an' all.

LIZZIE. God . . .

WILL. I'm just a weight round your neck. A dead weight. Go, you stupid woman. Go!

PHILLIPS. Oh my God. Oh my God.

*LIZZIE kisses WILL on the forehead and then runs away into they yard.*

Let me through. In the name of common humanity, let me through.

*PHILLIPS descends the rostrum steps into the audience.*

I'm a surgeon, don't forget. A doctor and a surgeon. Helped a good many of you draw your first breath. Brought a smile to your mother's face, I shouldn't wonder.

*He singles out a member of the audience.*

That's right, Dai Powell, I assisted your passage into this world, not twenty years ago. You wouldn't want to hasten my journey out of it, would you?

*Silence.*

I thought not. Let me pass.

*As he slowly makes his way out, a narrow prison bed is brought on and placed stage centre. As the stage transforms into the final scene, there is a reprise of the ballad, sung by a solitary male voice high up in the tiring-house.*

## Scene Twenty-Two

*Prison.*

*The stage is transformed into a prison. Rambling, ruinous – as much a prison of the mind as an actual place. The kind of prison engraved by Piranesi, with gantries, high walkways and hanging chains.*

BALLAD SINGER.
    In Newport town he was shot down,
    In a hail of shot and shell.
    His accomplice . . . she got clean away,
    But where to . . . none can tell.

*The stage area become a debtors' prison: the Marshalsea, where* MR BAINS *is now languishing. He lies on a narrow prison bed, shivering under a filthy blanket.*

Once locked up in a prison cell,
He told them his true name.
Confessed he to the murd'rous deed.
And then took all the blame.

*As the ballad comes to its conclusion, a* PRISON OFFICER *leads* WILLIAMS *onto the stage-right side of the upper level. He is made to sit in a chair. This now represents his cell.* WILL *is then led on in a similar fashion, sitting in the stage-left section of the upper level, which now represents the condemned's cell.*

For long and sleepless days and nights,
Their questions kept him busy.

The crime, he said, was his alone.
Not a word he said of Lizzie.

In court the boy stood not a chance,
They sentenced him to die.
And in the morning's cold grey light,
They said they'd hang him high.

PRISON OFFICER (*to* WILLIAMS). Threw the book at you,
didn't they? Hung, drawn and quartered. (*Spits*.) We don't
actually 'draw' you any more, you'll be pleased to learn . . .
slice out your vitals and hold the dripping offal up in front
of your eyes. What we do now . . . *before* we hang you . . .
what we do . . . we sit you on this hurdle – this little
wooden frame – and get a horse to *draw* it across the prison
yard. That way you'll be 'drawn' see? And the law's been
carried out.

WILLIAMS *looks up at him.*

Don't look at me like that. It ain't my fault you're in this
pickle. We've all of us got a station in life. And it's our
duty to remain within it. That way you've got a chance of
happiness. I've got a wife at home and three fine children.
Warm. Fed. Clothed. What more can a man want?

*A few* SHABBY FIGURES *drift about the stage below,
some pacing up and down like caged animals, others sitting
slumped against the wall.* MR BAINS *cries out in pain.*
MRS BAINS *tries to make him comfortable.*

D'ORSAY *pushes his way through a side door, holding a
small bunch of flowers to his nostrils. He is followed by*
ALDRIDGE *and* MRS HARRINGTON.

D'ORSAY. What a perfectly horrid place. A labyrinth of
dragging chains and echoing voices, so full of guilt and
remorse, the very brick is in a sweat.

MRS HARRINGTON *starts distributing small amounts of
food to the* PRISONERS *slumped against the wall.*

ALDRIDGE. Yes indeed. One half expects to open a door and
see a row of naked figures roasting over a sea of burning
coal.

D'ORSAY. A little cold for that, surely. Oliver Wadham, as I live and breathe. What on earth are *you* doing here?

WADHAM. I could just as easily say the same about you, y'know.

D'ORSAY. We're visitors, dear boy. Here at this good lady's invitation.

MR BAINS *cries out again in pain.*

WADHAM. Truth is, dear fellow, I lost a bundle on the gee-gees.

D'ORSAY. Word did get round.

WADHAM. And since the old patriarch is absolutely refusing to reach into his pockets . . . here I languish till the last trump sounds.

D'ORSAY. Know the feeling, old chap. Been pretty damn close to it myself.

WADHAM. It's not too bad, actually. I mean, one can always come and go. But it's always so terribly depressing turning oneself back in.

BETH, *now a young woman, hurries into the prison, accompanied by* JEREMY, *a young man in a stovepipe hat. She is carrying a small bunch of flowers.*

ALDRIDGE. Thought you worked for the Government.

WADHAM. Not any more.

ALDRIDGE. Always been under the assumption they took care of their own.

WADHAM. Not far enough up the ladder. Chaps at my level tend to be a touch expendable. Still, I always knew what the game was. I'm not complaining.

BETH *joins her mother at* MR BAINS' *bedside.*

BETH. How is he, Mum? Is he any better?

MRS BAINS. He'll be the better for seeing you, I expect. This young doctor came to see him this morning. He said to keep him warm and hope for the best.

BETH *gazes into* MR BAINS' *face, mopping his brow with a lace handkerchief.*

WADHAM. Tell the truth, dear boy . . . started to pale after a while . . . Heard chaps muttering about old Wadham going to the dogs . . . Soon realised I was a bit low on the old self-esteem.

ALDRIDGE. One did hear rumours.

WADHAM. Found myself wedded to the old claret jug . . . couldn't get through the day without it . . . Only a question of time, I suppose, before they asked me to walk the plank.

BETH. Hello, Dad. How are you feeling?

MR BAINS. Is that you, Lizzie?

BETH. No, Dad. It's me – Beth. No one knows where Lizzie is.

*She reaches for a tin mug standing on the shelf by the bed and cleans out the inside with her finger.*

I'll need some water for the flowers.

*She hands the mug to her mother, who takes the flowers and the mug and hurries out to get water.*

I ain't *selling* flowers no more, Mum. I'm *buying* 'em!

*By this time,* D'ORSAY *and* ALDRIDGE *have nodded their goodbyes to* WADHAM *and are both following in* MRS HARRINGTON's *wake as she administers to the inmates.*

The boy who done the murder were banged to rights. He's going to swing for it. Definitely. But they never laid hands on our Lizzie. We ain't heard from her in months. Ain't that right, Jeremy?

JEREMY *mumbles an inaudible reply. They make an incongruous couple. He is eighteen, trying to look like a man of the world, and she a child of fourteen, with rouged cheeks and a low-cut, red velvet dress.*

Dad, I've brought someone to see you. Say hello, Jeremy. He's my beau. We've got a little basement room in George Street. Life is just a whirl. I gets taken to the opera and all sorts. We goes dancing most nights, and I'm introduced to the most eligible fellows. And sometimes I does them a little favour. Just for sport.

*She takes her father's hand.*

Cheer up, Dad, you won't be here for ever. We'll see your debt paid off, won't we, Jeremy? Just as soon as them damn lawyers get his inheritance sorted out, we'll have money to burn.

*As* MRS BAINS *returns with the tin mug* (*now filled with water*) *she sees* MRS HARRINGTON *giving a drink to an* OLD DEBTOR *slumped against a column.*

MRS BAINS. I don't want to get in the way. But I'm Lizzie's mother. Remember? You came to see me a few months back.

*The* OLD DEBTOR *coughs weakly, dribbling down his front.*

MRS HARRINGTON. I did. Yes.

MRS BAINS. I just wondered if you'd heard anything of Lizzie.

MRS HARRINGTON. Not a thing.

MRS HARRINGTON *wipes the* OLD DEBTOR*'s mouth with a napkin and then moves on to an* OLD LADY, *sitting on the opposite side of the column.*

OLD DEBTOR. God bless you, ma'am.

MRS HARRINGTON. Such beautiful flowers.

MRS BAINS. They're for my husband. He's been in here for the past three months. Can't pay back what he owes. This awful place has quenched his spirits, Mrs H. (*Tearful.*) He's like to die, I shouldn't wonder.

MRS HARRINGTON. 'Like to die', you said.

MRS BAINS. Yes. I did.

MRS HARRINGTON. Was he not dying on the occasion of our first meeting . . . a good three years ago? It seems to be taking him an unconscionable time.

*Awkward silence.* MRS BAINS *arranges the flowers in the tin.*

MRS BAINS. Better be getting back.

MRS HARRINGTON. Your daughter had a heart of gold, Mrs Bains. I can't imagine what must've happened to implicate her in such a hideous crime.

OLD WOMAN. God bless you, Mrs Harrington.

MRS HARRINGTON. I wish I had something to remind me of her. A locket of her hair perhaps.

MRS BAINS. Can't help you there, ma'am.

MRS HARRINGTON *gets up and sets off for another part of the prison.*

MRS HARRINGTON. I won't rest until I find her.

BETH. Better be going, Dad. I got a number of engagements. (*Giggling.*) Very *lucrative* engagements. Ain't that right, Jeremy?

BETH *kisses her father on the forehead, then offers* JEREMY *her arm, and they start to walk out.*

We've got to go, Mum. I'll leave you to do the flowers.

*She hooks her arm into* JEREMY*'s and then flounces out.*

*On the upper level, a* PRIEST *is visiting* WILL, *on the morning of the execution.*

PRIEST. Is there anything you want to say to me?

WILL. I don't think so.

PRIEST. One last chance to unburden yourself before your soul is released on that final journey . . . when you must confront your Maker with your sins?

WILL. You don't frighten me, Reverend.

PRIEST. No man is wholly bad, in my view. You clearly have many good qualities . . . Loyalty not being the least of them – loyalty to one's friends. Perhaps even to one's King and country.

WILL. What are you driving at?

PRIEST. I've been instructed to say . . . that if you were willing to put a name to some of the more prominent of your Chartist contacts, over the past few months . . . then your sentence might well be commuted to one of life imprisonment – or even transportation.

WILL. What guarantee have I got?

PRIEST. A gentleman's word.

WILL. Not good enough, I'm afraid. Nothing doing.

*The* PRIEST *makes a gesture. The* HANGMAN *enters and* WILL*'s hands are bound. At the same moment, the* PRISON GOVERNOR *crosses to* WILLIAMS, *still seated on the other side.*

PRISON GOVERNOR. Mr Williams, I thought it only right to tell you, at this, the earliest convenience . . . that your sentence has been commuted to one of transportation. A compassionate decision, if I might say so. And a victory for common sense. You will be transported to the colonies, I believe, at some as yet unspecified time.

WILL *is pushed out through a rear door. At the same moment,* LIZZIE *enters below. She is wearing a dark dress and her face is partly veiled.*

MR BAINS. Lizzie! Is that you?

LIZZIE *stands at the foot of his bed.*

What did I tell you? I knew she'd come. I knew she wouldn't let her old dad down. You was always a good girl, Lizzie. You look after yourself. Don't go making the mistakes I made. Make a new start.

*He smiles.*

Get on a boat, girl. Say goodbye to the soot and the smoke. Set sail for new horizons. Somewhere under a bright sky . . . with good clean air . . . under the Southern Cross.

*There is crash from above as the ceiling trap opens and* WILL*'s body drops downwards, swinging on the* HANGMAN*'s noose.*

### Epilogue

*Summer 1869.*

*A room in a tavern in the Tottenham Court Road, opposite*
LOVETT*'s bookshop.*

LOVETT *slowly mounts the rostrum. He is nearly seventy*
*years old and not in good health.*

LOVETT. I've been asked to say a few words about the
London Working Man's Association, founded nigh on
thirty-five years ago, in a tavern much like this one, and not
very far away, if my memory serves me right. And as I look
around me, I can see one or two of the old faces, no doubt
able to share with me the memory of those early years.

*A murmur of affirmation.*

And though its life was a short one, our Association set
in motion an unprecedented period of social change in
this country: *radical* social change. Not in a tidal wave
of revolutionary upheaval, as many had hoped, but
gradually . . . like the steady drip of a tap, slowly filling
the cistern of our needs and drowning out the voice of
oppression and exploitation.

*Applause.*

Thanks to Mr Disraeli's very welcome and, I have to say,
most unexpected Bill of Reforms, much of what we fought
for is now in place. The worst of the corruptions within our
electoral system have at last been addressed. And, crucially,
every decent man in the country now has the right to vote.
But what Mr Disraeli has to understand is that we're not
asking for reform in the way that the beggar asks for a
handout from his benefactors; what we demand is an
equality of opportunity for every man, woman and child in
this country. And in that regard, there's still a way to go.

*He coughs painfully into his handkerchief.*

But there's no reason to be downcast, brothers and sisters, I can see a day coming when the working population of this country will no longer be held down in the shadow of ignorance, but released into the sunshine of a universal enlightenment. And on that day, our Parliament will be made up of men of all classes – *good* men – who will begin to mitigate against the evils of property and oppression. And devise the means by which prosperity and happiness shall at last gladden the face of our fertile land!

*He steps down.*

*The End.*

**Author's Note**

As *Holding Fire* was written with Shakespeare's Globe in
mind, the action of the play takes place not only on the stage
and in the musicians' gallery above the stage, but also in the
yard and the surrounding balconies.

To make the stage directions clearer, a brief description of the
theatre's interior would probably be helpful:

The stage juts out into a yard, where the audience can stand
and view the play on three sides. The rest of the audience are
seated behind them at ground level and on upper and lower
balconies, which again enclose the stage on three sides. At the
back of the stage there are three doors, through which the cast
can come and go, and twelve feet or so above the stage is a
gallery, which is referred to throughout the text as 'the upper
level'.

*Holding Fire* is written in broad strokes, covering a wide
sweep of history. There are several leading roles and a great
many characters, many more than is usual in a contemporary
play, where economic necessity often limits the writer to a
handful of characters and one set. This means that most of the
actors will have to transform themselves into a variety of parts.
If the story is to unfold as it should, these transformations will
have to be convincing.

Helen Edmundson
ANNA KARENINA *after* Tolstoy
THE CLEARING
CORAM BOY *after* Gavin
GONE TO EARTH *after* Webb
THE MILL ON THE FLOSS *after* Eliot
MOTHER TERESA IS DEAD
ORESTES *after* Euripides
WAR AND PEACE *after* Tolstoy

Karen Louise Hebden
A CHRISTMAS CAROL *after* Dickens

Edward Kemp
5/11
NATHAN THE WISE *after* Lessing

Ayub Khan-Din
EAST IS EAST
LAST DANCE AT DUM DUM
NOTES ON FALLING LEAVES
RAFTA, RAFTA…

Tony Kushner
ANGELS IN AMERICA – PARTS ONE & TWO
CAROLINE, OR CHANGE
HOMEBODY/KABUL

Owen McCafferty
CLOSING TIME
DAYS OF WINE AND ROSES *after* JP Miller
SCENES FROM THE BIG PICTURE
SHOOT THE CROW

Conor McPherson
DUBLIN CAROL
McPHERSON: FOUR PLAYS
McPHERSON PLAYS: TWO
PORT AUTHORITY
THE SEAFARER
SHINING CITY
THE WEIR

Arthur Miller
AN ENEMY OF THE PEOPLE *after* Ibsen
PLAYING FOR TIME

Mike Poulton
THE CANTERBURY TALES *after* Chaucer
DON CARLOS *after* Schiller
THE FATHER *after* Strindberg

Jack Shepherd
THROUGH A CLOUD

Nicholas Wright
CRESSIDA
HIS DARK MATERIALS *after* Pullman
JOHN GABRIEL BORKMAN *after* Ibsen
LULU *after* Wedekind
MRS KLEIN
NAKED *after* Pirandello
THE REPORTER
THERESE RAQUIN *after* Zola
THREE SISTERS *after* Chekhov
VINCENT IN BRIXTON
WRIGHT: FIVE PLAYS